BILL LAWRY

CHASING A CENTURY

Published in 2018 by Hardie Grant Books,
an imprint of Hardie Grant Publishing

Hardie Grant Books (Melbourne)
Building 1, 658 Church Street
Richmond, Victoria 3121

Hardie Grant Books (London)
5th & 6th Floors
52–54 Southwark Street
London SE1 1UN

hardiegrantbooks.com

Cataloguing in publications data available from the National Library of Australia
Bill Lawry: chasing a century
ISBN 978 1 74379 354 1

 A catalogue record for this
book is available from the
National Library of Australia

10 9 8 7 6 5 4 3 2 1

Publisher: Pam Brewster
Editor: Alison Proietto
Cover design: Luke Causby, Blue Cork
Internal design: Peter Daniel
Text layout: Kerry Klinner, Megacity Design
Managing Editor: Marg Bowman
Design Manager: Jessica Lowe
Production Manager: Todd Rechner
Colour reproduction by Splitting Image Colour Studio
Printed in China by Leo Paper Product. LTD

BILL LAWRY

CHASING A CENTURY

Hardie Grant

BOOKS

1ST INNINGS
ESSENDON
1ST INNINGS
514
OVER NO
LAWRY
282
BURN
0
EXTRAS
36
5 WKTS.
LAST WKT

CONTENTS

EARLY LIFE

NEIL HARVEY

I first encountered Bill Lawry when he was a kid at Preston Technical School. At the time, I was working at Lindsay Hassett's sporting goods store on Swanston Street in Melbourne's CBD and, when my cricketing commitments with Victoria and Australia allowed, umpiring games of school cricket in the summer and school baseball in the winter.

Bill represented his school at both sports, so I got the opportunity to watch him quite a bit from an early age.

It was obvious that he had a hell of a lot of ability in both sports. In cricket, he always had plenty of time to play the ball and he always wanted to go in to bat first. He was an attacking batsman and an excellent fielder. He was the standout player on every school team that he played in.

Bill visited the store fairly often to have a look at our baseball, and cricket gear. I always found him to be a likeable kid and I enjoyed chatting with him. It helped that we had a fair bit in common – we both played and loved cricket and baseball and we both batted left-handed. He had a good sense of humour. He liked a laugh. And he was mischievous in a good-natured way. When it came to talking cricket and baseball, he was honest and direct, saying precisely what he thought about the players and the game. So I wasn't at all surprised when some three decades later, he embarked on a successful career as a cricket commentator.

WISDEN

Born in the Melbourne suburb of Thornbury on February 11, 1937, Bill Lawry had no family background in big cricket. At the age of nine he took part in his first competition with Thornbury Presbyterian Church team; he spent three years in church cricket and also played for Preston Technical School.

The Australian district clubs set out to catch 'em young, and when he was 12 Northcote claimed him in their fourth grade side where he stayed two seasons, then one in the third, one in the second and at 16 he was promoted to the first. Thus he had eight summers in the senior grade before he toured England.

Lawry acknowledges the help he received from Jack Baggott, coach of the Northcote club. He greatly admires Australia's post-war left-handers, Morris and Harvey, although he did not try to copy their methods. Lawry is also a left-hander at winter baseball which has given him a splendid throwing arm. He also finds time to breed racing pigeons.

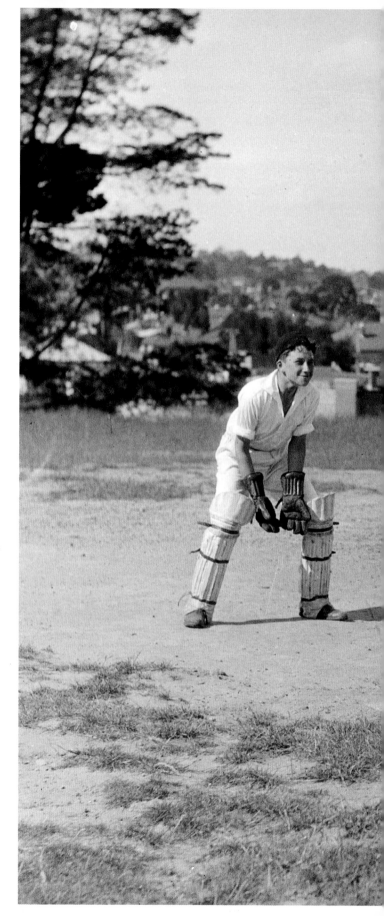

BOY PLAYING CRICKET IN THE 1950s.
(STATE LIBRARY OF VICTORIA)

BARRY MORRISON

We were both local lads, but because Bill went to Preston Technical School and I went to Northcote High School, we didn't meet until I joined Northcote C.C. Initially, I didn't play with Bill much because he was always a couple of grades above me.

A few years after I joined Northcote, I played against Bill for the first – and, as it turned out, only – time in my life. Victoria's Colts team took on a Victoria Combined Schools team coached by the legendary George Murray. Bill was in the former team and I was in the latter. Even then, it was clear that Bill had a lot of talent as a cricketer. He didn't have a lot of shots, but he had a very good defence. He was a resolute batsman, a brick wall who was able to stay at the wicket for long periods of time. He was slightly unusual for a left-handed batsman in that he didn't score a lot of runs off his pads through mid-wicket. His strength was his driving straight down the ground. As a tall, front-foot batsman, he met the ball with a straight full face. He was also an excellent outfielder with a good arm, honed through winters spent playing baseball.

I started to get to know Bill better in the mid-'50s when I joined him in Northcote's first XI and our parents joined a committee to provide the club's afternoon teas. Every week, our parents attended Northcote's home games and provided a home cooked selection of cakes and sandwiches for the players and umpires. I got to know Bill's parents very well. They were lovely people.

Their son was an amiable, albeit quiet bloke. He and I became friends. We didn't spend much time together socially outside of Northcote C.C., but we always knew what was going on in each other's lives because our parents worked so closely together on the club's afternoon teas committee. The thing which struck me about Bill was his very positive and determined attitude to cricket and life. That's never changed, and it's served him well over the years.

He didn't speak much, but when he did, his remarks were often sharp and witty. I liked that about him, and I wasn't at all surprised when he went on to become a very successful cricket commentator on TV. But back when we were teenagers, Bill's sharp wit sometimes didn't go over too well with some of our elders!

A FAMILY ENJOYS A DAY AT THE CRICKET TO WATCH A TEST MATCH BETWEEN ENGLAND AND AUSTRALIA. (FAIRFAX)

Tall for my age and skinny in frame, I walked a mile each day to attend the Wales St. State School, and at the tender age of eight years I made a nervous cricketing debut for the Thornbury Presbyterian Sunday School team. The competition was for boys up to 16 years of age and my activities were confined to batting at no. 11 and fielding in the most farflung positions. … At nine, I won the fielding trophy at the church's presentation evening.

— Bill Lawry

At Test match time, our whole family would troop off to join the swelling crowds waiting for the turnstiles to open at the Melbourne Cricket Ground. Once inside we would scamper for the prize positions in the southern stand behind the bowler. I would usually be first, my brother next, then Father, my sister and finally Mum, bringing up the rear.

— Bill Lawry

SPECTATORS WATCH THE ACTION DURING THE 1950–51 ASHES SERIES. (FAIRFAX)

16-YEAR-OLD GETS CHANCE

Sixteen-year-old batsman Bill Lawry will play for Northcote when the first district round starts tomorrow. Lawry played with Northcote Seconds last season. Northcote has also chosen 19-year-old Steve Kruger, who was in the Queensland Colts' team last year.

— *THE AGE*, 9 OCTOBER 1953

JOHNSON 1'17

Bill Lawry, 17, made 67 for Northcote against Fitzroy, He batted for 155 minutes, and had six 4's in his hand.

— THE *ARGUS*, 18 OCTOBER 1954

WRIGHT 143 N.O. IN DISTRICT CRICKET

Bert Wright (Footscray), with 143 not out, Bill Lawry (Northcote), 117, and John Edwards, 6/33 for St. Kilda, showed the best individual figures in District cricket yesterday when the third round ended.

— *THE AGE*, 3 NOVEMBER 1954

PENNANT LEADER IN DANGER

Carlton's 310 – best score of last week – looks too formidable for Northcote to cover. Young Bill Lawry, one of the best of the younger batsmen in pennant, is not out, and he is expected to be an important factor in Northcote's fight for the points.

— PERCY TAYLOR, THE *ARGUS*, 22 JANUARY 1955

Bill Lawry received a bad blow on the nose against Essendon but the damage was only superficial. The side played well together and Bill Lawry proved an able leader. His general handling of the team was commendable, while his general organisation of equipment and practice proved very helpful.

Preston Technical School magazine 1952

The Brunswick-Northcote bus. (Museums Victoria Collections)

*We lived in a terraced cottage in Thornbury, a northern suburb of Melbourne,
and the narrow concrete path that ran down our backyard to my brother's pigeon lofts
became my first cricket pitch. My father, who played cricket enthusiastically until
he was 51, and my brother, Ernest, who played for the Thornbury Baptist Church team,
bowled to me with a tennis ball from the moment I was big enough to hold a bat.*
— Bill Lawry

*I come from a poor working-class family. We had pigeons, chickens, dogs, ferrets.
We used to go rabbiting. We used to go fishing. That was our hobby. I used to play cricket in
the summer and baseball in the winter. My life has revolved around
my pigeons, my family, my cricket, my dogs. That's what we did. I didn't have
a motor car until I was 24.*
— Bill Lawry

March 53
2nd v Sand Mill.

BACK ROW HEN HOBBA ERN BARRY BILL LAWRY DOUG STEWART
L→R

FRONT ROW JACK PARRY DON GOUGH COL BRADLEY BILL LUDLOW
BARRY BROWN LOU BALCOMBE RON WERNECKI

NORTHCOTE TEAM PHOTOGRAPH IN 1953. (PROVIDED BY DOUG STEWART)

DOUG STEWART

A First-Class Maiden Century

Jack Baggott, a former captain and coach, invited Bill Lawry to join Northcote Cricket Club when he was 11 years old in the summer of 1948–49. Back then, a cricketer living in Bill's home suburb of Thornbury could choose to play for any one of three district clubs: Collingwood, Fitzroy or Northcote. Once he represented one of those clubs in the district competition, he was tied to that club.

Jack recognised Bill's talent and picked the 11-year-old for a few games in Northcote's third XI to tie him to the club.

Bill spent the next two summers – the summers of 1949–50 and 1950–51 – playing in Northcote's fourth XI before winning promotion to the third XI in the summer of 1951–52. I first met Bill Lawry in late January 1952 when I finished my national service in the army.

He was a quiet kid, but it didn't take long to see that he was also very strong-minded. He was already a very solid batsman, but being a skinny 14-year-old, he didn't have the physical strength to attack the bowling. He'd hit a well-timed on-drive and it'd go straight along the ground to mid-on for no run. He was, however, almost impossible to get out. As a kid playing in the lower XIs at Northcote, he'd bat nearly all day. He wouldn't make that many runs, but he'd stay there.

In those early days, Bill used to bowl a fair bit in the nets and sometimes, even in games. He bowled left-arm orthodox spin, although I must admit that I can't recall seeing any of his deliveries actually turn! His love for the game was evident. He always was a very keen cricketer.

Bill lived in the suburb of Thornbury – which is adjacent to Northcote – and usually caught the double-decker bus to training with Ernie Barry.

Bill rose steadily through Northcote's ranks. We played together during the summer of 1952–53 in the seconds. In March 1953, our scorer Col McKenzie took a team photo before our seconds game against South Melbourne. I still have the photo. More than half a century later, I showed it to him and asked, 'Who can you name there?' He named nine of his 10 teammates. Ernie, Bill and I are the three standing furthest to the right in the back row.

At the start of the next season, the summer of 1953–54, Bill made his first-grade debut for Northcote as a 16-year-old under the captaincy of the former Victorian right-arm quick Wally Dudley. They played University at University Oval on the second Saturday in October of 1953. He spent the first half of that summer batting in the lower-order and bowling a few overs.

In late January 1954, he was given his first opportunity to open the batting at first-grade level – keep in mind, he was still 16-years-old – and top-scored with 48 in

Northcote's competitive total of 232 all out against Carlton at Princes Park. He was retained as an opener – with the exception of Northcote's first innings against Prahran when he batted three – for Northcote's last three matches of the summer of 1953–54 but failed to reach 50 in any of his five innings, registering scores of 6, 4, 35, 9 and 6.

Fortunately, our selectors kept faith with Bill and the breakthrough soon came. In Northcote's second match of the following season, the 17-year-old Bill scored 67 and 44 not out against Fitzroy at the oval which would one day bear his name, and followed that up with 117 against Richmond at Punt Road. I remember those two games well, as they were the second and third games of my brief first-grade career. I made my first-grade debut almost by accident in Northcote's opening match of the season. I was named 12th man and a local lad by the name of Jim Beitzel who lived around the corner from Westgarth Street Oval was named in our XI, having put in a request to transfer to Northcote from Fitzroy. He had a last minute change of heart, so I was called into Northcote's first XI at short notice.

I made a decent start to my first-grade career, scoring 41 and 1 not out batting at nine and eight in our season opener against Essendon at Windy Hill, and 37 batting at eight against Fitzroy at home. In the latter game, I hit a lofted drive over the bowler's head and Jim Beitzel (the player I had replaced), caught me on the fence at long-off. Bill batted beautifully for his 67 in our first innings against Fitzroy. He drove straight and authoritatively. He backed that up with an unbeaten 44 in our second innings which staved off outright defeat.

Our next game was against Richmond at Punt Road. Bill, still only 17, didn't have a driver's licence. I was 21, but didn't own a car. Don Gough, our wicket-keeper, used to give Bill, Stan Fisher and me a lift in his great big Chev. Don, like more than a few keepers, was small in stature and we used to wonder how his feet reached the pedals in that Chev!

On the way to games we would ask Bill, a pigeon fancier, how they knew who won the race. Bill would demonstrate that there is a ring on their leg and when they arrive home you take the ring off and put it in a special, tamper-proof timing clock to measure their time of arrival. After about three or four weeks asking the same question, Bill realised we were just having a bit of fun.

Richmond batted first and declared overnight on the imposing score of 7/328. Wally Driver made a hard-hitting even hundred, hitting Len McMenamin for a towering six which landed inside the members' bar.

Bill opened with Don and I batted eight. By the time I walked out to join Bill in the middle, we were 6/183 and Bill was unbeaten on 97. Doug Ring, a leg spinner who was one of Bradman's 1948 Invincibles and had played the last of his 13 Tests just over a year earlier, was bowling to me, having just removed our captain Wally Dudley for 27. I played out Doug Ring's over and Bill faced the next one, bowled by another of Bradman's 1948 Invincibles, Bill Johnston, a left-armer still playing Test cricket for Australia, who alternated between fast-mediums and finger-spin.

Johnston was bowling his fast-mediums. Bill (Lawry) flicked him out to deep mid-wicket and we scampered to try and get the three runs that would take Bill to his maiden first-grade century. Doug Ring, who was by then 36 years old, chased down the ball and threw it to the keeper's end as I was running in to complete the three. I made my ground, but the ball bounced awkwardly and grazed the side of my head. I looked up the other end and was happy to see that Bill had reached his hundred. I shook off the blow and faced up to the next ball from Johnston who promptly clean bowled me for a duck! Still, I'm happy to say that I played a part in getting Bill to his maiden first-grade hundred.

Two months later, Bill made his second XI debut for Victoria at Adelaide Oval. Bill made a duck in his only innings that game and had to wait 11 months for another opportunity in Victoria's Second XI. He made it count, scoring 183 against South Australia's Second XI at the Junction Oval in late November 1955. Bill completed his national service in the air force in early 1956 and in mid-February he made his Shield debut for Victoria as an 18-year-old, opening the batting alongside Colin McDonald.

THIS IS CRICKET

Bill Lawry, 6ft. and 18 year-old Northcote left-hander, is batting himself into consideration by State selectors. He made a most attractive 55 not out against St. Kilda yesterday.

— The *Argus*, 2 November 1955

WHAT A DAY!

Cricket in Melbourne on Saturday was certainly a day for the record books. Deadly bowling by Arthur Day and Arthur Dean, of Footscray, enabled them to share all 20 wickets lost by Northcote in the District cricket game at Northcote. In the middle of all this devastating bowling, young Bill Lawry, only 18, made 51 in 89 minutes with good all-round cricket.

— The *Argus*, 28 November 1955

WE'RE STILL HUNTING FOR THOSE BRIGHT TEST HOPES

I went eagerly to St. Kilda yesterday hoping to find a youngster who could walk straight into the Australian Test team. But I went home disappointed. There was not a star in sight. However, today that youngster could show up. Most likely candidate is Bill Lawry, 18-year-old left-hander, of Northcote. There was merit in his 43 not out as Victorian opener. But he must adopt a different technique when he resumes today. His innings yesterday was patient, sound, unspectacular. We know he can play the shots, and he would delight us if he played those shots – and demonstrated a more aggressive outlook in his batting. Just toward the end of play he showed signs of aggression, only to close up to make sure of getting another start today.

— Percy Taylor, The *Argus*, 30 November 1955

PERCY TAYLOR

He has flaws to conquer, but ... Cricket finds a brand new star

A new cricket star was born at St. Kilda yesterday. Bill Lawry, tall young left-hander from Northcote, shrugged off the anxiety that once clouded his batting, and scored a brilliant 183 for Victoria's 2nd XI against South Australia. His great knock put Victoria in a winning position, brought new fame to Lawry – and a glow of satisfaction to me.

I went to the match on the first day looking for Test match prospects, and, although I left the ground disappointed, I wrote that Lawry was promising. Yesterday Bill fulfilled that promise – and how! Based on a firm defence, his play was much more confident, and he unwound a succession of strokes all round the wicket. Not for a moment do I think he will walk into the Australian eleven, but we saw enough to indicate that he has distinct possibilities. For one thing he showed us yesterday that he has a really sound defence. On top of that he played some really nice on-side shots, particularly a leg glance, a sweep to leg, and some well-timed on-side placements. One stroke I admired a great deal. It was a short-pitched ball outside the off-stump, and Lawry most adroitly got on top of it to speed it to the fence without giving the slips men a chance. Now I want to see him concentrate on well-timed, firmly played cover and off

drives, and I would not be dismayed if I saw him lifting the ball over the head of mid-on.

So now I suggest to him that he should practise a little more aggression. At the moment he has a slightly bunched-up attitude in his stance. I would not worry about that over-much – except that it probably prevents free stroking of the ball. But – Bill's lack of strength cannot be criticised too much. He is only 18, and has probably outgrown his strength. When he becomes more set we could see a real batsman. Indicative of his cricket ability was the fact that, after reaching his century, he went on, calmly and unhurriedly, to strive for another. Don Bradman and Bill Ponsford had the same attitude when they had reached three figures.

— The *Argus*, 1 December 1955

NORTHCOTE OPENER'S BILL LAWRY AND DON
GOUGH GO OUT TO BAT. (NEWSPIX/HERALD SUN)

VICTORIAN TEAM

RICHIE BENAUD

From *Willow Patterns*

I first saw Lawry in 1956, oddly enough in a tied match, the first such game in which I ever took part. He opened the innings this day with Colin McDonald and his performances hardly set the Yarra afire, for Davidson picked them up for 1 in the first innings of that game and he was LBW to Alan Wyatt in the second innings for 7. He wouldn't have made any impression on me at all except that Colin McDonald told me later he thought Lawry, who was out of form at this time, was a future Australian opening bat. The season before, Lawry had played in one match and made only 3 and in this current 1956–7 season he made just 248 runs at an average of 20 for Victoria and the only batsmen below him in the Sheffield Shield averages were bowlers. McDonald said that Lawry was one of the straightest players he had seen and was possessed of a good temperament and, in years to come, he would make his mark in the game.

I was just 17 years of age and my debut for the Victorian Second XI produced a humiliating duck. … Tour manager Les Ferguson told me not to worry. There would be plenty more chances, he forecast. But when you are 17, it is hard to take the wise, long-range view.
— Bill Lawry

RICHIE BENAUD IN 1956 WHILE TOURING ENGLAND.
(BARRATTS/PA IMAGES VIA GETTY IMAGES)

YOUNGSTERS GRABBED THEIR CHANCE

Although former Test opener George Thoms made a solid 100 for Melbourne, it was a group of teenagers who stole the day in pennant cricket on Saturday. And it was not an easy day. Rain affected wickets, and caused up to five adjournments during the afternoon. Bill Lawry, up and coming left-hander, saved Northcote with an unfinished 52 in a score of 5/100. Following his 183 for Victoria seconds last week this tall 18-year-older will soon force the selectors to take notice.

— THE *ARGUS*, 5 DECEMBER 1955

POWER OUT – LAWRY IN

Fast-bowler, John Power, last night was dropped from the Victorian team and young Northcote opening bat, Bill Lawry, replaced him. Victoria will play Western Australia at the St. Kilda Cricket Ground tomorrow. Selectors decided that, because of the injury to John Shaw, it was necessary to bring in another opening batsman into the State side. Lawry, a tall 18-year-old left-hander, from Northcote, pleased everyone with a grand 183 for the Victorian seconds against the South Australian seconds in December. Since then he has built a little more aggression on to his undoubtedly strong defensive game.

— THE *ARGUS*, 9 FEBRUARY 1956

SELECTORS WORRIED.
THEN ALONG CAME BILL...

State selectors breathed a sigh of relief when young left-hander Bill Lawry walked into Northcote practice last evening. He could not be contacted all day to advise selectors if he was available to play with Victoria today. Bill, who is doing his National Service training with the R.A.A.F. at Laverton, told Northcote officials he had been given leave to play. This is Lawry's Shield debut, and could be the beginning of a really good career for this left-hand batsman, who is only 18.

— PERCY TAYLOR, THE *ARGUS*, 10 FEBRUARY 1956

One afternoon while drilling on the RAAF parade ground, I was handed an urgent telegram which read: 'Have you seen this morning's paper – Mum'. I was given permission to break off and hustled to a newspaper stand where the morning headline read: 'Bill selected but doesn't know'. Aircraft recruit (minor) 313053 was chosen in the Victorian Sheffield Shield side. My big chance. Fortunately our adjutant was favourably disposed towards cricket and when I asked for leave it was promptly granted.
— Bill Lawry

BOB SIMPSON

The old scorecards tell me that the first time I encountered Bill Lawry was when Western Australia played Victoria at the Junction Oval in mid-November 1956. Bill was 19-years-old and playing in just his second first-class game. To be honest, I can't remember a thing about that match!

I do, however, have a very clear memory of Bill batting at the WACA for Victoria against Western Australia in late November 1959. He made 70 and 50 not out in a drawn Shield match. Playing for Western Australia, I remember watching him closely in both those innings and being intrigued by how this 22-year-old Victorian opener could concentrate so well. At that early stage of his career, he wasn't scoring very quickly, but it was clear that he was going to be a very, very good player in the future. During that match, we said g'day to each other, but that was about it. We lived on opposite sides of the country, so we weren't mates yet.

NEIL HARVEY

The teenage Bill just kept getting better and better every year and, in mid-February 1956, he broke into the Victorian team as an 18-year-old, opening alongside Colin McDonald. The next summer, the summer of 1956–57, the Victorian selectors gave Bill an extended run in the side and I took over the Victorian captaincy from Sam Loxton, who graciously stepped aside to give me a shot at the Australian captaincy which had become vacant with the retirement of Ian Johnson.

After eight Shield matches, we dropped him from the Victorian side, because he just wasn't scoring enough runs. In 13 innings, he'd only managed 251 runs at an average of 19.31. Bill copped his dropping on the chin. I knew that he'd be back. By the time Bill returned to the Victorian team as a 21-year-old in mid-January 1959, I'd moved to New South Wales. In his second coming as a Victorian cricketer, I faced him for the first time in early February 1959 at the SCG. Bill scored 14 and 64 not out to help Victoria secure a draw. He'd clearly improved as a batsman. He was more positive, more willing to take on the bowling. I was very impressed.

By the end of that summer, he'd established a foothold in the Victorian team. In five matches, he scored 361 first-class runs, including four half-centuries, at an average of 60.16. He backed that up the following summer, the summer of 1959–60, with 666 runs, including one century and five half-centuries, at an average of 41.62. The following summer, the summer of 1960–61, was a crucial one for all Australian cricketers, because there was an Ashes tour in 1961. Bill had a great summer for Victoria scoring over 1000 first-class runs, including two tons and five half-centuries, and was picked for his maiden Test tour at the age of 24.

Bill was opening regularly for Victoria, but struggling to score runs. He was, at least, occupying the crease and taking the shine off the ball. The press, however, started criticising him for being too slow. One evening at Northcote training, I just happened to be walking off the oval directly behind Bill and our coach Norm Dickson. Norm told him, 'Bill, I think you'll have to start getting more aggressive with your batting in the state side. You'll get dropped [if you don't]'.

'Norm,' replied Bill, 'I've played like that to get in and I'll play like that to get out.' And he did. And the Victorian selectors dropped him in early March 1957 after his eighth Shield game. But, after spending nearly two years out of the Victorian team, he fought his way back in and established himself as one of the finest openers that Victoria and Australia have ever had.

Like I said, he always was a strong-minded fella.
— Doug Stewart

SPECTATORS WATCH A CRICKET MATCH
IN VICTORIA IN THE EARLY 1960S. (FAIRFAX)

LAWRY PUNISHES N.S.W. ATTACK TO SCORE 266

Consistent Victorian batsman Bill Lawry scored 266 to put his team in a strong position in their match against N.S.W. at the Sydney Cricket Ground today. Lawry's 266 is the highest Individual Sheffield Shield score since the war and the highest first-class score in Australia this season. Rohan Kanhai previously had the distinction of the best innings this year with 252 against Victoria in Melbourne.

— *Canberra Times*, 3 January 1961

KEITH STACKPOLE

The first time that I really had anything to do with Bill Lawry was when we went on a Victorian tour of Tasmania together in January 1960. Bill was 22 and had finally established himself as one of Victoria's first-choice openers after being dropped and spending nearly two years out of the team. I was 19 and hadn't played a single first-class game.

Back then, Tasmania had first-class status, but they weren't playing in the Sheffield Shield, so the Victorian selectors dispatched a semi-second-XI team composed of younger members of Victoria's Shield XI such as Bill, fringe players trying to break back into Victoria's Shield XI and youngsters like me who'd yet to experience first-class cricket.

The 22-year-old Bill struck me as a fairly dour sort of bloke, an introvert who didn't drink and went to bed early. In January 1960, none of us state players were professional cricketers, but Bill behaved like one. He was a good teammate who was just totally dedicated to cricket. I quickly learned that everyone on the Victorian team called him 'the Phantom' or simply 'Phanto'. He had a lovely, quirky sense of humour, but he didn't express it nearly as often as he would later in life. He was tall, he was lanky and as a batsman he had a beautiful defence.

I played my first two first-class matches on that tour of Tasmania, but I wouldn't play for Victoria again for over two years. It was during that period that Bill established himself as one of the finest opening batsmen in Australia. As a young batsman trying to break into the Victorian team, I followed his career with great interest.

With an Ashes tour scheduled for the winter of 1961, the summer of 1960–61 was a crucial one for all Australian cricketers. The 23-year-old Bill produced the best summer of his career, scoring over a thousand first-class runs at an average of 54.84. He clinched his spot in Australia's Ashes touring party with a mammoth 266 against New South Wales at the SCG.

PLAYING FOR
AUSTRALIA

RICHIE BENAUD

From *Willow Patterns*

It was in 1960–61 that Lawry gained his chance when, at a moment where three or four openers were vying for a place in the Australian side to tour England, he made 266 for Victoria against New South Wales in Sydney. He had been dropped at 12 in that game and, despite his double century, his choice was something of a surprise in the touring side.

His first-class form in Australia had been such that he was dropped from the Victorian side in 1957–58 and in part of 1958–59 but thereafter his studious concentration and wide variety, though not always seen, and range of stroke-play ensured him a prominent place in Sheffield Shield and Australian teams.

CHANCE FOR LAWRY TO MAKE TEAM

Victorian opening batsman Bill Lawry now has a chance of making the Australian team for the fourth Test against the West Indies starting in Adelaide on January 27, which will be named on Thursday.

With the failure of several batsmen, notably Favell and Mackay, Lawry could make his Test debut at Adelaide. Lawry has the second highest batting aggregate in Sheffield Shield matches so far this season. Neil Harvey is leading Shield batsman. Lawry was Victoria's best batsman in Sheffield Shield last year and looks like repeating his performance. With scores of 266, 85, 83, 66 and 44 so far in interstate games this season, Lawry has a far better average than some players in the Test team.

— *Canberra Times*, 19 January 1961

BARRY MORRISON

Bill acquired his nickname of 'the Phantom' in his very first second XI game for Victoria as a 17-year-old in late December 1954. The nickname quickly filtered back to Northcote and stuck. We all called him that and still do. Even now, when we chat to one another about his latest escapades on telly, we'll say, 'the Phantom is doing this' or 'the Phantom is doing that'.

I can still vividly recall the Thursday evening in mid-February 1961 when I heard the wonderful news that the 24-year-old Phantom had been picked for the Ashes tour later that year. When I arrived at Northcote training at Westgarth Street Oval, someone said to me, 'Aw, the Phantom's gotten into the Test side'. The Phantom himself – a plumber by trade – was a bit late to training that evening, because he'd been busy working on the plumbing at Melbourne's new Royal Children's Hospital.

I congratulated him as soon as he arrived. 'Well-deserved', I told him. Obviously, he was happy to be picked, but he remained very composed. We talked about what his aims were for the 1961 Ashes tour. At that stage, 25-year-old Bob Simpson and 32-year-old Colin McDonald were well-established as Australia's opening partnership, having enjoyed a productive and successful home summer against the West Indies. Thus, to the outside world, it looked like the Phantom had been picked for the tour as the young spare opener. He didn't quite see it that way. Of course, he respected both Simpson and McDonald, but he resolved to put his head down and score a lot of runs on the tour. By doing so, he believed that he could win a place in Australia's Test XI. Like I said, Bill always had a positive and determined attitude to life.

THE AUSTRALIAN CRICKET TEAM ARRIVES IN ENGLAND IN 1961.
BILL LAWRY IS FAR RIGHT. (TRINITY MIRROR/MIRRORPIX/ALAMY)

GRAHAM McKENZIE

We were two of the younger lads in the touring party. I was 19 when we left Australia by ship; Bill was 24. Neither of us had played a Test.

The ship journey over to England was a wonderful experience. I got to know all my Australian teammates before we played a single game together in England. I barely knew any of them when our touring party was picked. In 1961, Western Australia was still pretty isolated from the rest of the mainland states.

Every morning on the ship, we got up early and did a physical training session before breakfast. If memory serves, it was voluntary for the first two weeks during which we had about a half dozen regular attendees, then compulsory thereafter. Brian Booth was PE teacher and I'd just finished training as a PE teacher, so we ran the sessions. It was just about the only time that I got to use my training as a PE teacher. The first two days of my nascent teaching career had fallen on Shield days – so I took leave to play – and on the third day, the press showed up and told me that I'd been picked in Australia's 1961 Ashes touring party. After that, I became busy playing Shield, Test and county cricket.

When we got to Malta, the British press got onboard to snap some photos of us. We thought we'd better give them a decent show, so we padded up and had a net session onboard the rolling ship.

35

CYNTHIA STRACHAN

Born in 1937, Bill Lawry is 6ft 2in, weighs 12 stone, has been a regular opening batsman for Victoria for three years, and has played for 12 years with Northcote, the grade team he now captains. Bill learned his cricket mostly from his father, Alf Lawry, who is still an enthusiastic social cricketer, but he [Bill] also owes a lot of his skill in the field to baseball. When Test cricket tours don't interfere, he's a keen baseballer who pitches and fields first base for the Collingwood baseball team. Away from sport, his hobby is racing pigeons, and this is a field in which he's as successful as he is at pounding a cricket ball. He began this hobby when he was just 12, and now keeps 50 birds in the loft of his parents' home. Not long before the cricket team sailed for England, his pigeons won seven Federation races in Victoria and a Victoria-to-Tasmania race.

Bill, who makes batting look easy, even though he's not the most elegant of stroke-makers, is known among the Aussie team as the 'Phantom'. And, as any English bowler will tell you, it's an apt name, for he's always striking back with a vengeance.

A non-smoker and teetotaller, he celebrated his score of 165 against Surrey by drinking half a gallon of milk in The Oval dressingroom. Unfortunately for the feminine cricket fans, there's one Joy in Bill Lawry's life that he loves more than Test cricket. She's his fiancé, Joy Barnes, and on his return from England they'll be house-hunting in readiness for their marriage next year.

— *AUSTRALIAN WOMEN'S WEEKLY,* 26 JULY 1961

At the beginning of the Australian cricket tour of England for the Ashes, two schoolboys admire a bat containing the signatures of Aussie captain Richie Benaud and his team. (Birmingham Post and Mail Archive/Mirrorpix/Corbis via Getty Images)

SECOND TEST OF THE ASHES SERIES, AUSTRALIA'S
BILL LAWRY IS HIT ON THE GLOVE BY A FAST
DELIVERY. (S&G/PA IMAGES VIA GETTY IMAGES)

ROLAND PERRY

From *Captain Australia*

[Lawry] was forced to wait longer than most for a break into the big time of Test cricket. His name was not whispered loudly as a Test chance until the 1960–61 season, when Australia was doing battle with the West Indies and was well served by openers Colin McDonald and Bob Simpson (and before him, Jim Burke).

Lawry in that season scored a massive 266 in a 'defiant' innings (according to Victorian journalists – New South Wales journalists described it as 'painstaking') against New South Wales. It was enough to be chosen for the 1961 tour of England.

Everyone expected McDonald and Simpson to open in the Tests. They had shown courage above and beyond the call against Hull. They had earned their stripes and spots. But form in cricket is a season by season thing. The only way to break into the Test team is to make so many runs that you had to be considered. Lawry was twenty-four as the boat sailed and he knew that he had to make it on the trip or be relegated to state cricket for another five years and oblivion.

Lawry batted first on tour in the second game against Yorkshire and scored just 29. It was back to the old firm of McDonald and Simpson for game three. Then it was on to the 'big' county game for the Australians, versus Surrey. This team had crushed Australia embarrassingly in the corresponding game of that awful tour of 1956. Lock and Laker had been the destroyers, with Alec Bedser not even needed. That game had set a pattern of

decay from which the tourists never recovered. This time, there was a lot of pent-up feeling about facing Surrey at The Oval. Bedser and Lock were still in the side, but Laker had retired. Yet they were just names now, older and less potent.

Lawry took control from the first over of the game and wiped out fears for Benaud and his team about past disasters. He hooked, pulled and drove his way to a century in three hours. He crunched 101 between lunch and tea. Lawry was out half an hour after tea for 165. Benaud could declare at seven for 341 and then dismiss the county twice with ease. Australia won by ten wickets.

The lanky opener followed this up with a century against Cambridge University. The selectors could sniff something special in his form. They ran him for the third game in a row against Glamorgan. He hit 31 and 43 not out. His form was holding. Benaud was smiling. Instead of struggling to find a batsman on fire as in 1956 and 1953, he had everyone functioning on most cylinders. Benaud was like a billionaire with a furrowed brow over how to earn another few million. It was an embarrassment of batsmen. He left Lawry out of the

LAWRY IN CENTURY STAND FOR AUSTRALIA

A great lightning century by Victorian batsman Bill Lawry put Australia in a strong position at the tea adjournment of the second day's play in the second Test match against England at Lord's.

Lawry's century was the highlight of a dogged rearguard action by batsmen, who fought their way from being two wickets down for six yesterday to five for 191 at tea. The tea-time total was only 15 runs behind the England first innings score. Lawry, usually a dashing batsman, played in an unfamiliar role as he struggled to put Australia's innings back on a firm footing after a disastrous start yesterday. He was at the wicket for four hours, and 40 minutes before reaching his hundred. His innings included 15 fours. He fought hard for every run and received a great ovation from the large crowd when the 100 runs were posted. He was again cheered from the field when he left with Alan Davidson for the tea adjournment. Lawry is playing in only his second Test match.

FIFTH 100

His century yesterday was his fifth of the tour and easily his most valuable. When he reached his hundred, Lawry, who opened the innings with Colin McDonald yesterday, had kept one end intact while five teammates lost their wickets. He figured in an invaluable partnership of 95 with Queenslander Peter Burge, who is also unaccustomed to this 'backs to the wall' cricket. His fifth wicket partnership with Burge is the highest ever made by a visiting team at Lord's. The previous best was the 87 partnership between Keith Miller and Bill Brown on the 1948 tour of England.

Lawry's century also:
- Included a fighting 75-run partnership with captain Neil Harvey.
- Is the first century scored by a visiting batsman in a Test at Lord's since South African Roy McLean's in 1955.
- Is Lawry's second century at 'headquarters' in two matches this tour.

The Victorian survived some uncomfortable moments in reaching his hundred. He played several streaky shots, particularly against the pace men, but gave no real chance.

— *CANBERRA TIMES*, 24 JUNE 1961

next game but made sure he played at Lord's against the Marylebone Cricket Club on 27 May. This was an important game. The Marylebone Cricket Club would field a near Test side. Australia did the same. Opening with McDonald (24), Lawry made his first appearance at the world's most famous ground and made 104. Just to show he wasn't dazzled by his own form, he settled in for a powerful 84 not out in the second innings, this time with Simpson (92 not out), as Australia cruised to a ten-wicket win.

Benaud's thinking was obvious. It wasn't now a question of Lawry opening in the first Test, it was a matter of with whom – McDonald or Simpson. In the final two games against Oxford University and Sussex before the Tests, Lawry hit 72, 12 and 30. McDonald was given the job of starting the innings with his fellow Victorian. Simpson's form had been very good too. He made the team batting at number six. Lawry made a creditable start with 57, about ten above what would be his career average. Australia amassed nine for 516 and the game was drawn.

It was on to Lord's. England won the toss, batted and was held to 206, thanks to Alan Davidson's sensational display of left-arm swing and bounce. He took five for 42. Lawry pushed his nose down over a lowered bat handle to keep the tricky bounce on the Lord's ridge under some sort of control. He was 32 not out at stumps, with Harvey on 6 not out. The next day, Lawry played the innings of his life. His temperament came to the fore on one of the most difficult wickets ever seen in a century of big cricket at Lord's. There would be no century in a session on this Friday of 23 June.

Australia moved from four for 111 at lunch to five for 183 when Burge (46) was dismissed. Lawry was on 99 not out. He clipped a single off Statham to reach his first Test century in his second innings. He went on to 130 and was the match winner. No one else scored more than 66. Australia won by five wickets.

Lawry made another century – 102 – again the only one in the vital fourth Test at Old Trafford.

Bill Lawry's series aggregate was 420 at 52.5. On tour he hit nine centuries out of his 2117 runs. Lawry had left Australia a spare opener and had come back a Test hero. His decade-long career at the top was under way.

LAWRY HITS UP SIXTH CENTURY

Australian opener, Bill Lawry, hit his sixth century of the tour against Lancashire today. Lawry scored 122 before being caught off Statham. Lawry's previous centuries were against Surrey, Cambridge University, M.C.C. Kent and England. His century today took his tour aggregate to 1230. Australia were 3/305 at tea in reply to Lancashire's total of 346. Lawry figured in another opening century stand with Bob Simpson.

CANBERRA TIMES, 4 JULY 1961

My first memory of Bill Lawry is huddling up in my bed as a 12-year-old in our family home in the beachside Adelaide suburb of North Glenelg, listening to the ABC's radio commentary of the 1961 Ashes tour. Believe it or not, Bill was a dasher and it was exciting listening to the commentators' descriptions of his aggressive stroke play. Australia won the Ashes 2-1 and the 24-year-old Bill was the young batting find of the tour, scoring centuries in both of Australia's Test victories.
— Greg Chappell

BILL LAWRY IS RUN OUT BY ENGLAND WICKETKEEPER JOHN MURRAY FROM A THROW BY GEOFF PULLAR DURING THE FOURTH TEST IN MANCHESTER. (EVENING STANDARD/GETTY IMAGES)

RUN HUNGRY AUSSIE

It's still anyone's guess how the scoreboard will look at the end of the current England–Australia Test-cricket series. But the Australian team is much more confident of its prospects since it found it can call on a brilliant young plumber to get it out of difficulties – Bill Lawry, the 24-year-old Victorian. And if Bill's sudden rocket to cricketing fame is making him laugh like a newly mended drain, you couldn't blame him. For the boy who is our cover pin-up this week was one of the boys some cricket critics cried should be left behind when the Australian side sailed for England. The tall, sharp-featured Lawry landed almost unknown on the cricket fields of England, but the cricketer few Englishmen had heard of suddenly became the cricketer on every Englishman's lips. He became news as far back as May, when he played against Surrey at The Oval and scored 165 runs, becoming easily the highest scorer for the tour at that stage. Denis Compton, England's former batting cavalier, was full of praise for the new star, stating that he 'had not seen such shots (as Lawry's pulls and hooks off anything short of a length) played so ferociously since the great days of Bradman'. So Lawry won his way into the First Test, and gave a performance becoming a veteran. But it was in the Second Test at Lord's that he really became a cricketing great. On a treacherous wicket that had the world's best batsmen struggling to make double figures, he cracked a brilliant 130 runs and paved the way for an Aussie victory. His 130 in the Second Test brought his tally in two months in England to 1024 runs and five centuries, and sent every cricket statistician thumbing through the record books. The statisticians couldn't remember such a run-hungry Aussie, and their record-books backed up their memories. Bill, a quietly spoken young man who lives in the Melbourne suburb of Thornbury, took all this in his stride, shyly raising his bat in acknowledgment.

CYNTHIA STRACHAN, *AUSTRALIAN WOMEN'S WEEKLY*, 26 JULY 1961

RICHIE BENAUD

From *Willow Patterns*

I didn't know him very well early in 1961 and on board ship on the way over he was a very quiet member of the team. He and Frank Misson turned out to be the practical jokers of the side and all the young players came under the influence of Ken Mackay who was the oldest member of the team, and one of the quietest himself – he made sure they were well looked after with picture shows, Chinese food, television and early nights.

He [Lawry] has never admitted it, but I have long suspected him as a prime mover in the nailing of the Australian captain's shoes to the Sydney dressing-room floor, at a time when I was to appear at a Government reception. Rumour had it in 1961 that, when Australian manager Syd Webb found some solid silver in his pocket walking across the drawbridge of a stately castle and had to return them red-faced, Lawry or Misson had a hand in it.

But I will never forget him for his effort in Brisbane in 1963 after Ian Meckiff had been called for throwing. I hadn't bowled Meckiff from Lou Rowan's end after he had been called by umpire Egar in the early part of the match and feeling ran high in Australia over the whole question. Reports appeared in the newspapers that police protection was being offered to the umpires and I had wryly thought that no one was offering any to the captain. Worse still, play was washed out on the Monday and, seated in the luncheon room next to the dressing-rooms, I was musing on life in general when suddenly the team masseur appeared before me. He was dressed in masseur's clothes with plastic raincoat on top and a hat pulled down over his eyes, and was carrying a copy of the pink *Melbourne Sporting Globe* over one hand. The paper asked in screaming type why I hadn't bowled Meckiff

from the other end and also in big type carried the story of police protection being needed.

Jock, the masseur, when I looked at him had the whites of his eyes showing and he said, 'Why didn't you bowl him from the other end?' 'Go away', I said, 'I have got enough problems …' He whipped the paper away to show he had a gun in his right hand and said, 'You should have bowled him from the other end'. All those old stories about your life flashing in front of your eyes are quite true, I can assure you, and he then pulled the trigger, producing a flash from the barrel of the gun. It took me two seconds to realise I hadn't been hit with anything and a wave of relief swept over me until I caught sight of this figure rolling around on the floor outside the luncheon room. It was Lawry, completely overcome by the success of one of the best planned practical jokes of a cricket lifetime.

He can take a joke as well as give one, a fact that makes him one of the outstanding team men with whom I have ever toured. I put the 1961 tour down as the most pleasant I have undertaken and there were a variety of reasons for this. Not least of these was Lawry's presence in the side, both as player and team man, and the team spirit he and others like Misson, Mackay and their tight knit group were able to foster for Neil Harvey and myself.

SUBBA ROW DROPS BILL LAWRY OFF
FRED TRUEMAN'S BOWLING IN THE
FOURTH TEST AT OLD TRAFFORD IN
1961. (TRINITY MIRROR/MIRRORPIX/ALAMY)

The Australian Cricket Team, 1961.
(PA IMAGES VIA GETTY IMAGES)

BOB SIMPSON

Throughout the course of the summers of 1959–60 and 1960–61, Bill kept piling on the runs and his reputation in Shield circles grew and grew. It came as no surprise when, in the autumn of 1961, Bill was picked for his maiden Test tour, the 1961 Ashes, at the age of 24. At 25, I was only a year older than Bill, but by that stage, I'd already been playing Test cricket for over three years and Colin McDonald and I had established ourselves as Australia's Test opening partnership.

The long journey by ship to England in 1961 was when I first got the opportunity to really get to know Bill. Our captain, Richie Benaud, and our vice-captain, Neil Harvey, made sure that we were a team on the ship. We all sat together for meals and we practised or had physical training twice a day. We all bonded quickly. Harv was fantastic with youngsters coming into the side. He'd known Bill since he was a teenager and was his first Victorian captain. With Harv's help, Bill and the other new players soon settled in.

The first thing that I learned about Bill was that no-one in the team ever called him 'Bill'. Everyone called him 'Phanto'. He'd gotten the nickname in his very first second XI game for Victoria as a 17-year-old in late December 1954. The Vics were playing South Australia at Adelaide Oval and Bill arrived at the train station in Melbourne carrying a stack of magazines, including some *Phantom* comics. Victoria's captain, Dick

Maddocks, quipped, 'I see we've got a *Phantom* fan. We'll call him the Phantom'. From then on, he became known as 'Phanto'. The nickname filtered very quickly through Australian cricket and it's what we still call him today. It's an unusual nickname and a good one.

Phanto and I were about the same age and we were both non-drinkers. So we got along well. We and the other younger players in the touring party – such as Brian Booth and Graham McKenzie – soon started knocking around a bit together. No matter where we were, we talked cricket all the time. We just loved cricket and couldn't wait to embark on the challenge of beating England on their home soil.

If you only meet Phanto briefly, you could walk away with the misimpression that he is a staid sort of bloke. But once you get to know him, you quickly realise that he has a wonderful sense of humour. That helped him settle into the team very quickly. He's just great fun to be

Glory for the Brave Lawry.
— the London headline in the Daily
Mirror

England need men of the courage of storm-
trooper Bill Lawry if we are to save this
Second Test. Gum-chewer Lawry dug in
behind that Lord's ridge at 5.33 p.m. on
Thursday night and endured 6 hours
9 minutes of non-stop shelling from our fast
bowlers.
— Brian Scovell, Daily Sketch

William the Conqueror.
— Yorkshire's Bill Bowes, 1961.

around. He's mischievous in a good natured way and his pranks help keep the team's mood happy and positive on a long boat trip and overseas tour.

Once we arrived in England, Phanto's tour took off with a 165 against a good Surrey attack featuring Tony Lock and Eric Bedser at The Oval in mid-May. I remember thinking to myself: geez, this bloke's even better than I thought he was! That was the innings that made everyone look up and say, 'Hey, this bloke can really play'.

Phanto soon established himself as our form batsman on tour. Twelve days before the first Test at Edgbaston, he batted beautifully at Lord's, scoring 104 and 84 not out against the MCC. It was clear then that he was a real chance to make his Test debut in the first Test at Edgbaston.

Australian cricket has got a proud history of making sure that young people that are succeeding get a lot of opportunities and I was very happy for Phanto when he was subsequently picked for the first Test. He took the news in his stride. He was never the sort of bloke to jump all over with excitement when he did well or got some good news. He's a calm, self-contained cricketer who always keeps his emotions under control. That's what made him such a great Test opener.

Richie handled the change in our batting line-up smoothly and diplomatically. 'You know,' he explained to me, 'Phanto's done very, very well on tour. Colin has played as an opener for a long while. You've done well as an opener too, but we think you can also do the number six spot well for the team.'

As usual, Richie soon looked like a genius. In Australia's first innings of the first Test at Edgbaston, Phanto got 57 on debut and I got 76 batting at six. That Test ended in a draw. In the second Test at Lord's, Richie was injured, so Harv captained Australia for the first and only time. This turned out to be a crucial Test which became known as the 'Battle of the Ridge' after the distinct protrusion at the Nursery End of the ground which was later revealed to be the top of a drain that had been laid under the pitch years earlier. England's captain, Colin Cowdrey, won the toss and batted. His side made 206 in their first innings. Alan Davidson was superb, taking 5/42. In reply, Phanto scored his maiden Test century, 130 in 367 minutes, to lead Australia to a commanding first innings lead of 134.

It was a wonderful knock. Phanto just kept on going, even as wickets fell around him. Remarkable really, for a bloke playing in just his second Test. And it was to prove a match-winning knock as we won by five wickets with over a day to spare to take a 1–0 series lead over an England team who hadn't lost in 18 Tests. Phanto took his success in his stride. He didn't change at all. Internally, I reckon that early part of the tour probably made him realise just what a good player he was.

People sometimes ask me if I can remember any shots that Phanto played in his maiden Test century at Lord's. The truth is: I can't, because Phanto wasn't the type of batsman who played memorable shots. He had his own style of batting, he knew what it was and he stayed within its perimeter. That's what made him such a great Test opener.

England won the next Test at Headingley to square the series 1–1 with two Tests to play. The series was decided and the Ashes retained in the fourth Test at Old Trafford. Richie, back from injury, won the toss and batted on a green seamer. Colin McDonald succumbed to a wrist injury so Phanto and I opened together for the first time. Our first innings together didn't go so well. We only put on eight before I nicked off to Brian Statham. Phanto soldiered on and his 74 in an innings when no other Australian batsman reached 50 steered Australia to a semi-respectable first innings total of 190. England responded with 367 for a first innings lead of 177.

In Australia's second innings, Phanto and I put together our first century opening stand: 113. I was cross with myself when I nicked one from Jack Flavell to be dismissed for 51. I thought we could've put on 200 together! From the very outset, we ran well together. We pushed the ball around and constantly took quick singles to rotate the strike and keep the scoreboard ticking over. It always gave us a quiet sense of satisfaction to see the opposition getting poopy about it. Bowlers, especially opening bowlers, hate not being able to bowl at one batsman for an entire over.

Lawry, Lawry Hallelujah! Yes, the tall, thin man of Australia, Bill Lawry, with a beak like Disney's perky doll Pinocchio, trod the glory road at Lord's yesterday.
— Brian Chapman.

Lawry is one of the best players of fast bowling I have ever seen.
— Bill Bowes, writing in 1961

Each time I see Lawry, the more convinced I become that he is going to be one of the biggest thorns in England's side for years. He had a century on his first appearance at The Oval, a century on his first appearance at Lord's and today he looked set for a century in his first Test.
— Sir Leonard Hutton during Lawry's first Test tour of England

Our positive running between the wickets just happened naturally. We never explicitly discussed it before walking out to bat together. It helped that we were both big, loud callers. We made a call nearly every time that we got a run and as we passed one another in the middle of the pitch, we'd say 'one', 'two' or 'three'. That clear communication is crucial to successful batting. There were many occasions when a good early call from Phanto saved me or vice versa. We were both firm believers in the importance of backing up at the non-striker's end. Once the ball was in play, we liked to be at least a couple of yards down the pitch at the non-striker's end.

Now, back to Australia's second innings at Old Trafford in 1961. Phanto, playing in just his fourth Test, made his second Test century: 102 in 268 minutes. By the time he was dismissed, he'd helped Australia turn a 177 run first innings deficit into a 97 run lead with seven wickets in hand. Then Richie famously went around the wicket and took 6/70 to bowl Australia to a 54 run victory. We held the Ashes, so we retained the urn by taking a 2–1 series lead with one Test to play. Phanto had played four Tests and scored two match-winning centuries. I remember thinking how extraordinary and impressive his performance was, especially since I'd played 15 Tests and hadn't scored a single century!

Australia drew the fifth and final Test at The Oval to win the series 2–1.

RICHIE BENAUD STRIKES AND ENGLAND'S TED DEXTER IS CAUGHT FOR 76 DURING THE LAST DAY OF THE FOURTH TEST AT OLD TRAFFORD. (DENNIS OULDS/CENTRAL PRESS/GETTY IMAGES)

Bill Lawry in England in 1961.
(NATIONAL ARCHIVES 8832095)

NEIL HARVEY

Bill settled into the Australian team very quickly on and off the field. He and the New South Welsh fast-medium bowler, Frank Misson, were always pulling good-natured pranks. They gave our tour manager nightmares! Once, at a formal dinner, Bill deftly placed some knives and forks in our unsuspecting manager's pockets. The poor fella looked as though he was pinching the cutlery!

Any experienced Test cricketer will tell you: you need blokes like Bill and Frank in your team. Their pranks and sense of fun keep the team's spirits up on long overseas tours away from home. Without them, it's very easy for team spirit to fall into a rut that's hard to get out of.

As the Australian vice-captain, I was a selector on the 1961 Ashes tour. At the start of the tour, we saw Bill, one of three openers picked in the touring party, as our spare opener. After all, Bob Simpson and Colin McDonald were already well-established as Australia's opening partnership.

But Bill soon started mounting a persuasive case for Test selection. In our early tour games, he batted aggressively and scored a mountain of runs. The game against Surrey at The Oval in mid-May stands out in my memory. He scored 165 and hit Tony Lock, England's left-arm orthodox spinner, straight back over his head. The next week, he scored 104 – his third first-class century of the tour – and 84 not out against the MCC at Lord's just 12 days before the first Test at Edgbaston.

We picked him to make his Test debut at Edgbaston not just because of the amount of runs he'd scored on tour, but the manner in which he'd scored them. He had a positive attitude and went after the bowling. Bill opened with Colin and we moved Bob to six. Bill made 57 in his first Test innings and Bob made 76. The Test ended in a draw.

In the second Test at Lord's, our captain Richie Benaud was injured, so I had the privilege of captaining Australia for the first and, as it later turned out, only time. This Test became known as the 'Battle of the Ridge' because there was a ridge running across the pitch on a good length at the Nursery End, which was later revealed to be the top of a drain that had been laid under the pitch years earlier.

England's captain, Colin Cowdrey, won the toss and batted. I let Alan Davidson bowl into the ridge and he was superb, taking 5/42 to restrict England to 206. Then Bill, playing in just his second Test, played what I believe to be his greatest Test innings. The ridge was making life extremely difficult for batsmen. If the ball pitched on the bowler's side of the ridge, it could rear up and hit the batsman between his eyes, but if it pitched on the batsman's side of the ridge, it could shoot through and hit the batsman in the ankle. By the time that Bill was dismissed after tea on the second day, he'd scored 130 of Australia's total of 7/238 and had the bruises to prove it. In his six-hour plus stay at the crease, he'd copped numerous blows on the body from Fred Trueman and Brian Statham, the finest fast bowling partnership that England had ever produced.

Thanks largely to Bill's 130, we took a commanding first innings lead of 134 and seized control of the Test, eventually winning by five wickets with over a day to spare. It was a great win. Those of us who drank, celebrated by getting stuck into the Veuve Clicquot. Bill, of course, was a non-drinker, but he didn't need to drink to be the life of the party!

BILL LAWRY HEADS AUSTRALIAN RECOVERY

Opener Bill Lawry, with a superb century, headed a great Australian fightback against England in the fourth Test today.

Lawry with the temperament of a Test veteran, scored 102 to help Australia to 3/252 at tea. After trailing England's first innings score by 177, Australia had a lead of 75. With his hundred today, Lawry notched his eighth of the tour and second of the Test series.

When Lawry reached his 50, he had passed the half-century for the fourth time in the Test series. His Test scores have been: 17, 130, 1, 28, 28 and fourth Test (first innings) 74. Australia resumed this morning still 114 behind.

FOUNDATION

Simpson and Lawry, with an opening stand of 113, laid the foundation for Australia's recovery.

— *CANBERRA TIMES, 1 SEPTEMBER 1961*

GRAHAM McKENZIE

I first encountered Bill Lawry when I made my Sheffield Shield debut for Western Australia at the MCG as an 18-year-old in mid-February 1960. Bill opened for Victoria alongside Colin McDonald and got a few runs – 127 and 38 not out – to help his team to a 10 wicket win. I remember being impressed by his batting technique and style, but I didn't really get the chance to get to know him off the field.

A year later, Bill and I were picked for our first Test tour, the 1961 Ashes. That was when I got to know Bill. We were roommates on the ship and throughout most of the tour once we arrived in England. We were young and just happy to be on the tour. As you can imagine, we talked a lot about cricket! Bill's love for the game shone through. I remember waking up some mornings and seeing him standing there in front of the mirror in his underpants practising a few shots. Gee, I thought to myself, there's a dedicated cricketer!

The one foreign conversation topic that I had quickly to get up to speed on was pigeons. Bill was already an avid pigeon fancier and loved chatting about his birds. I must confess that when he first started talking about them, I hadn't a clue what he was on about. But he soon educated me!

Once we arrived in England, Bill soon started performing exceptionally well. His breakout performance came against Surrey at The Oval in mid-May. Bill scored a fairly dominating 165. That really got him noticed. It also started a trend on tour of Bill scoring hundreds on Saturdays. Precisely two weeks later, on his first visit to Lord's, he scored a 104 against the MCC at the home of cricket.

Now, in those days, Sunday was always a rest day, even if we were in the middle of a game. Bill had many an enjoyable Sunday on that tour. He'd order all the Sunday newspapers and start his day by reading about his Saturday run-scoring feats over breakfast. Then he'd head out to spend the day with his fellow pigeon fanciers. Word had gotten out that he was a pigeon fancier and our tour itinerary was on the public record, so local pigeon fanciers were always getting in touch to invite him to have a look at their pigeons when he was in town. He loved it!

BILL LAWRY INTERVIEW WITH SIDHARTH MONGA

Pigeon-racing has been in my family. My father was a pigeon fancier. My brother, who was 14 years older, was a pigeon fancier. So from the day I was born, there has always been pigeon love.

I am not sure if you understand pigeon-racing. It's a sport that is very strong in places like Belgium and Poland and England. Becoming very popular in China and Japan. It was the sort of sport that was probably at its peak before the First World War. Everybody - particularly, in England, the miners – had a pigeon love. When I toured, particularly in England and South Africa, where pigeon-racing is very strong, when we didn't play on Sundays I would go out pigeon-fancying. The Queen in England, she has got the pigeon love. She doesn't obviously do [pigeon-racing], but she has got the pigeon love. George Duckworth, the former England wicketkeeper way back, was a pigeon fancier. Sir Gordon Richards, the famous England jockey, was a pigeon fancier.

It's a sport you are born into. I have been very lucky. I have made a lot of friends away from cricket through pigeon-racing.
— Bill Lawry

GRAHAM McKENZIE

I was excited for Bill when he was picked to make his Test debut in the first Test at Edgbaston. I didn't play in that game, but I was happy just to be there, watching. Since the WACA wasn't a Test venue yet, it was only the second Test match that I'd ever watched! The only previous Test that I'd seen was the tied Test against the West Indies at the Gabba nearly six months earlier when I happened to be in Brisbane with Western Australia for a Shield game that started a couple of days after the Test, so we were able to attend the final day of the Test as a team.

I watched from the balcony as Bill made a composed 57 and the first Test was drawn. The second Test, played at Lord's, is one that I remember well. It was the first Test that Bill and I played together. I made my Test debut as a 19-year-old and had the privilege of opening the bowling with the great Alan Davidson. I can still remember running in and bowling the first ball of the Test from the Nursery End.

We bowled England out for 206. Davo bowled beautifully, taking 5/42. Bill, playing in just his second Test, was the mainstay of our innings. He scored 130 to lead us to a total of 340 and a first innings lead of 134. His innings was the difference between the two teams' first innings totals. He batted really well on a pitch that wasn't easy to bat on. There was a ridge running across it at the Nursery End and bowlers operating from the Pavilion End targeted the ridge mercilessly.

During the change of innings, our stand-in captain for that Test, Neil Harvey, came up and told me that, in England's second innings, I'd be bowling from the Pavilion End into the ridge at the Nursery End. In England's first innings, Davo had operated from the Pavilion End and I'd operated from the Nursery End. Given that Davo had taken 145 Test wickets to my one, no-one would've batted an eyelid if Harv had given Davo use of the Pavilion End in England's second innings too. Instead, Harv chose to treat me and Davo equally. He really was a fair-minded bloke. Both Harv and Davo were

THE SPECTATORS ENJOY THE ASHES
SERIES AT LORD'S CRICKET GROUND
IN ENGLAND IN 1961. (KEN KELLY/
POPPERFOTO/GETTY IMAGES)

tremendously supportive when we walked out there. They told me that I didn't have to do anything different from what I normally did – the ridge happened to be right on my natural length. It was good advice. I took 5/37 and we won the Test by five wickets to take a 1–0 series lead.

England won the third Test at Headingley to square the series. The Ashes was decided in the fourth Test at Old Trafford. Richie Benaud won the toss and batted on a green seamer. Unfortunately, we were bundled out for 190. Bill's 74 in an innings when no other Australian batsman reached 50 averted complete disaster. Still, when England responded with 367 for a first innings lead of 177, we were in deep trouble.

Bill and Bob, opening together for the first time in Test cricket, had only managed eight in the first innings before Bob departed, but in Australia's second innings, they turned the Test with an opening partnership of 113. Bill, playing in just his fourth Test, continued on to his second Test century, a 102 in 268 minutes with 13 fours. By the time that he was dismissed before tea on day four, we'd turned a 177 run deficit into a 97 run lead with seven wickets in hand. His innings gave us the opportunity to be in the game. We ended up making 432 in our second dig, setting England 256 to win in three hours and 50 minutes.

When England reached 1/150, with Ted Dexter on 70-odd and scoring at nearly a run a minute, we thought the Test was over. Then Richie came around the wicket, Dexter nicked a hard cut shot and Wally Grout took a great catch. We removed the remaining eight English wickets for the addition of just 51 runs. Richie finished with 6/70 and we won by 54 runs.

It was just an amazing match to be a part of. Our whole team was thrilled. We'd pulled off one of the most unlikely wins in Australia's Test history. Bill had made a huge contribution with his twin innings of 74 and 102.

Lawry's first tour was his finest. His aggregate of 2,019 was third behind Bradman and Harvey post-war, and has never since been equalled. He scored another Test century at The Oval, after which Bill Bowes wrote: 'Lawry is one of the best players of fast bowling I have ever seen.' With experience going back to Bodyline, Bowes knew his onions.
— Malcolm Knox from The Captains

A VIEW OF LORD'S CRICKET GROUND IN ENGLAND
DURING THE ENGLAND V AUSTRALIA ASHES SERIES IN 1961.
(KEN KELLY/POPPERFOTO/GETTY IMAGES)

The Australian team walks out onto
the field during the Ashes series in 1961.
(TRINITY MIRROR/MIRRORPIX/ALAMY)

NEIL HARVEY

After Lord's, England won the next Test on a doctored pitch at Headingley to square the series 1–1 with two Tests to play. The series was decided and the Ashes retained in the fourth Test at Old Trafford and Bill, playing in just his fourth Test, made a vital contribution. Richie won the toss and batted on a green seamer. Bill's 74 in an innings when no other Australian batsman reached 50 steered Australia to a semi-respectable first innings total of 190. England responded with 367 for a first innings lead of 177.

In our second innings, Bill brought up his second Test century, a match-winning and Ashes-retaining 102 in 268 minutes with 13 fours. It was a hell of a good innings against a strong English attack comprised of Fred Trueman, Brian Statham, Jack Flavell, David Allen and Ted Dexter. By the time that Bill was dismissed before tea on day four, we'd turned a 177 run deficit into a 97 run lead with seven wickets in hand.

I remember watching Bill and Bob from the balcony that day. They were very, very good together. They called loudly and ran well. I wasn't surprised when they went on to become our best opening partnership since Arthur Morris and Sid Barnes. Bill had scored two match-winning centuries in his first four Tests and although Bob had yet to score the Test runs to do justice to his ability, we knew what a good player he was and that it was simply a matter of time before he started converting his starts into big Test hundreds.

On the final day, Richie famously went around the wicket to target the footmarks created by Trueman and Flavell's follow-through and took 6/70 to bowl Australia to a 54 run victory. In the space of two days, we'd turned a 177 run first innings deficit into a 54 run victory. It was probably one of Australia's greatest ever wins in Test cricket and Bill, playing in just his fourth Test, had played a crucial role.

We celebrated a bit in the dressing room with a few quick beers, but our celebrations didn't last too long – we had to catch the train to London that night. We drew the fifth and final Test at The Oval to win the series 2–1.

KEN PIESSE

From *Dynamic Duos: Cricket's Finest Pairs and Partnerships*

If it wasn't for a brand new Mini Minor van with a stiff gearshift, Bill Lawry's celebrated pairing with Bobby Simpson at the head of the Australian order would have been delayed at least 15 months.

Australia's senior opening batsman Colin McDonald developed such a sore wrist from changing the gears of a new car during the 1961 tour, he could barely hold a bat. Reserve opener Bobby Simpson had played each of the first three Tests down the list and was promoted to the top of the order with McDonald unavailable for both the fourth and fifth Tests. McDonald had bought the car for his wife Lois and young daughter Karen who, with the assistance of Ashes stalwart Alec Bedser, were renting an apartment in Nightingale Lane, Clapham.

'The wives weren't allowed to be in the same hotel as the players back then', said McDonald. 'Alec organised this apartment for us and, to help ferry Lois and Karen around, I bought this Mini Minor. I was lucky to get it as the demand for vehicles was far greater than the production, but it had this very stiff gear shift which I could only just move, so much so that I developed a repetitive strain in my left wrist, my top hand (which controls the bat). By the end of the Leeds Test (the third of five, when McDonald made 54 and 1) I could hardly hold a bat and stood down from the last two Tests. I stayed on after the tour to work in the UK and never played another Test. I wish to goodness I'd never got that car! But it was the start of the Simpson-Lawry union

and my injury also saw Brian Booth come into the side for the first time. He was to become a very fine player for Australia.'

The McDonald-Lawry stands in the first three Tests in 1961 had been worth just 27 per innings. Lawry and Simpson flourished from their first Test together at Old Trafford, sharing an important second innings stand of 113 before Richie Benaud famously went around the wicket and spun a revitalised Australia to the Ashes.

It was the first of nine century stands by the pair, including five against the old Enemy, their daredevil running between wickets an immediate characteristic.

Don Bradman and the Australian selection panel always favoured a left- and a right-hander at the head of the order and the Simpson-Lawry combine was a pivotal force in Australia's top-order for five consecutive summers, home and away. Their judgment of the short single always seemed impeccable, ladies in the crowd often screaming as the pair stole ever-so-short singles, despite having just tapped the ball a yard or two in front of their feet.

'We'd call, but not always, especially if we defended at our feet,' said Lawry. 'We always reckoned the safest place to be was at the non-striker's end and we'd do everything possible to get there.'

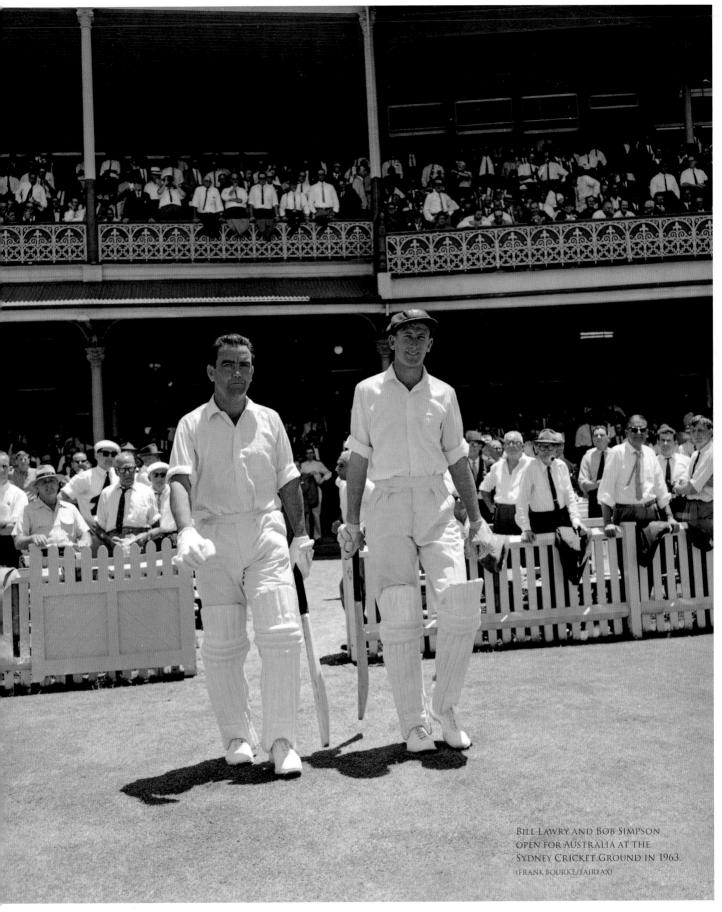

BILL LAWRY AND BOB SIMPSON
OPEN FOR AUSTRALIA AT THE
SYDNEY CRICKET GROUND IN 1963.
(FRANK BOURKE/FAIRFAX)

BILL LAWRY AT ARUNDEL IN APRIL 1964.
(BOB THOMAS/GETTY IMAGES)

WISDEN

Cricketers of the Year 1962

A comparatively unknown 24-year-old cricketer who came to England with Richie Benaud's 1961 team made the strongest impact of any post-war Australian batsman on his initial tour. He was William Morris Lawry, a member of the Northcote Cricket Club in Melbourne and of the Victoria State eleven. As a Test left-handed opener he established himself as successor to Arthur Morris.

It was ironical that this tall, lean young man with the sharp jaw, who stood six feet two inches, bore the nickname 'the Phantom' bestowed upon him when he first joined the Victoria team and his colleagues discovered his youthful addiction to a comic strip character of that name.

As he went from one triumph to another Lawry, with his slight crouch at the wicket, his long reach to kill the spin, was very much there in the flesh in the eyes of the England bowlers.

Presenting a really straight bat, he combined a well-organised defence with a satisfying, if not very wide, range of strokes, showing readiness to hit the loose ball and extraordinary facility in placing it.

Admirable composure and power of intense concentration supplemented these assets. He was stout hearted, stubborn or pugnacious as circumstances prescribed, and had the temperament of being able to carry on unruffled by error.

One of eleven newcomers to England in the Australian party, Lawry topped the batting with 2,019 runs, average 61.18 in first-class matches and 420 runs at 52.50 an innings in the five Tests. Also he hit most

centuries, nine. Only Don Bradman, 2,428 runs in 1948, and Neil Harvey, 2,040 in 1953, among Australians also made over two thousand runs in England since the war.

That the summer was mostly fine after the first week did not detract from the left-hander's glory. He hit a century in each of the two Tests that Australia won: 130 on the exacting ridge at Lord's and 102 in the Test which decided the Ashes at Old Trafford after 74 in the first innings.

Lawry, the raw recruit, soon adapted himself to English pitches, which he found slower than those at home but with more pronounced spin and cut. He had been sent to England as a promising opener – solid and with strokes developing. His sole major achievement had been 266 – after being dropped at 12 – in a punishing innings for Victoria against New South Wales in Sydney shortly before the Australian selectors chose the team for the tour.

During the early days of the tour, O'Neill, Harvey and Burge each scored a century for the Australians before Lawry got his first in England at The Oval. It was a dominating innings against Surrey on a Saturday in

*Gaunt and gawky as an electric pylon,
Lawry never had a chance to become
a stylist. He settled for results … Spectators
in England may walk out on him;
Hillites in Sydney may jeer. He is consoled
by his run account. Bill Lawry is a one-man
army of occupation, extorting an endless
toll from the enemy. Such men as Kanhai or
O'Neill or Barber play precariously exciting
innings; runs settle on Bill Lawry like
barnacles on an old ship.*
— *John Arlott,*
English radio commentator

OVATION

The crowd just finished applauding Lawry for his magnificent century when they began to give him a wonderful ovation at the end of his innings. Two balls after he had smacked the boundary to reach 100, Lawry played a tentative stroke at a ball from Allen. Trueman, fielding close in on the leg side, took a simple catch and Australia was 3/210.

CANBERRA TIMES, 1 AUGUST 1961

May; also it was one of the most significant of the whole season. It was a flowering of technique and temperament and it opened many English eyes and many Australian eyes, too.

In four and a half hours, Lawry scored 165 out of 286. He produced powerful drives beautifully placed past cover or mid-off; he hooked hard and he pulled hard. He pounced on anything loose offered by Test spinner Tony Lock. Denis Compton said he had not seen such ferocious hooking since the days of Bradman. Lawry had arrived.

As at The Oval, he hit a century on his first appearance at Lord's, 104 against M.C.C., and was shaping for a second, 84 not out, when the closure was applied. On his Test debut at Edgbaston he made a good impression with a steady innings of 57. Since The Oval it had been obvious that Lawry would open in the Test though it meant splitting an established pair, McDonald and Simpson.

Lawry was Australia's spinal column in the second Test at Lord's. This was an indomitable effort of sheer graft under severe pressure with the ball flying about and he was tenacious, painstaking and wonderfully cool. He took bruising blows. True, he made some passes at fiery Trueman and Statham, but he stuck it out for six hours, hitting the loose ball cleanly and placing it well. That innings of 130, his fifth hundred of the tour, gave Lawry one thousand runs inside two months.

After the Old Trafford Test, W.E. Bowes, a former England pace bowler, wrote that 'Lawry was one of the best players against fast bowling I have ever seen'. In the later stages of the tour some staleness was evident and his batting lacked previous composure and colour, but the fact remained that the tall one's batting did expand on his baptismal tour.

Returning to his own country, Lawry promptly became the Victoria captain. A popular character, modest, staunch and intelligent, he is a splendid team man.

BOB SIMPSON

By the end of that 1961 Ashes tour, Phanto and I were opening partners and good mates. Over the next two and a bit years, we established ourselves as one of the best opening partnerships in the world. We complemented one another. I batted right-handed, he batted left-handed. I was a fairly attacking batsman, whereas he was a bit more circumspect. And if we both wanted the same thing, we'd share without being asked, for example, as openers, we both liked to take strike, so we took it in turns. We never drew up a written rota or anything. We were just so comfortable with one another that each of us instinctively knew when it was our turn to take strike.

People were a bit surprised when, upon taking over the Australian captaincy from Richie in early January 1964, I chose to break up the Simpson–Lawry opening partnership, moving myself down to three and installing 22-year-old debutant Ian Redpath as Phanto's new opening partner for the second Test against South Africa at the MCG.

My reasoning behind that move was simple: by that stage, Phanto and I were very experienced Test cricketers. It wouldn't have mattered to either of us where we batted. We were keen to get Redders into the team – he was young and scoring lots of runs for Victoria opening alongside Phanto. We thought that if we let Redders bat in his usual opening position on his Test debut, he'd be more relaxed. He and Phanto proceeded to make me look good on my captaincy debut by putting on 219 for the first wicket.

In the winter of 1964, I had the privilege of leading Australia on an Ashes tour for the first time. The English press labelled our touring party 'the worst team ever to come out of Australia'. No surprises there – they've done that nearly every time that we've gone over there! Young Redders was deservedly picked in our touring party and in the first two Tests at Trent Bridge and Lord's, I chose to give him the opportunity to open alongside Phanto and moved myself down to six. Those first two Tests were drawn and the Lawry–Redpath opening partnership didn't really take off. From the third Test onwards, I restored the Simpson–Lawry opening partnership and moved Redders down the order.

We won the third Test at Headingley to take a 1–0 series lead which we never relinquished. Phanto and I, in our first innings back together as openers, put on 50, then Peter Burge walked in at four and smashed 160 off 308 balls to give us a match-winning first innings lead of 121. In our second innings, Redders, batting at three on a

THE AUSTRALIAN TOURING CRICKET TEAM, LED BY CAPTAIN BOB SIMPSON, ARRIVE AT HEATHROW AIRPORT IN 1964. (CENTRAL PRESS/HULTON ARCHIVE/GETTY IMAGES)

sluggish, turning pitch, made a vital unbeaten 58 off 174 balls to steer us to the victory target of 109 with seven wickets to spare.

In the next Test at Old Trafford, I won the toss and didn't hesitate to bat on a pitch which resembled a motorway. With the English sun uncharacteristically shining on our backs, Phanto and I put on 201 for the opening wicket – a new Australian record against England. Just after 4pm on the first day, Phanto skipped down the pitch – which he didn't do often – to the English off-spinner John Mortimore, middled a straight drive along the ground and instinctively ran. Unfortunately for Phanto, Mortimore made a great stop. I called out 'no' and ducked back into my crease. I looked up and suddenly saw that Phanto was still coming my way! It all happened in the blink of an eye. He was run out for 106 off 313 balls. I must confess that it was one of the worst stuff-ups that we ever had! If it hadn't happened, I genuinely believe that we could've put on 400 for the opening wicket at Old Trafford in 1964.

Phanto later copped flak for his slow scoring in that Test. I thought that that was very unfair. He's always been a good team man and he was only doing what I'd instructed him to do – bat conservatively, as we only needed two draws to win the series. We comfortably drew that Test at Old Trafford and the final Test at The Oval to win the series 1–0. Not bad for 'the worst team ever to come out of Australia'.

When I stood down as Australian captain in early January 1968, I was very happy to learn that Phanto would be my replacement. I didn't give him any advice about the job. He didn't need any. By that stage, he'd become a great Test cricketer and a great mate.

It was a privilege and a pleasure to play alongside him.

ROLAND PERRY

From *Captain Australia*

Show pain, no gain

When Lawry was hit by a bouncer, spectators would take bets on when he would rub the spot or flex the shoulder. On principle – he had a rule never to show weakness to a foe – Lawry would never react when struck. Usually a few overs after the hit, the 187-centimetre, lean opener with a prominent nose would roll his shoulder or give the bruise a quick rub.

It was the 1950s and 1960s when budding cricketers were taught by coaches never to show they had been hurt, even if a hand was too numb to hold the bat or if an elbow was aching. It was a time without helmets, armguards, painkillers, or the magic spray to anaesthetise welts. John Wayne, James Bond, Ron Barassi and Bill Lawry were macho heroes. It was a male sin to show pain and, heaven forbid, cry.

Lawry made 2,019 runs on that 1961 tour and was the only player to pass the 2,000 mark, with the highlight of his career, the maiden Test century at the home of cricket on a pitch which later was found to have a 'ridge' at the Nursery End.

This Test pitch, when Lawry walked out on the second morning, was anything but a good strip. Lawry was magnificent. He was also black and blue by the time he came back to the dressing room, having made his maiden Test century and batted six hours and ten minutes in all. When he went, at 238, he had made 130 and although over the years he played other splendid innings, for me there was nothing to match his first hundred at Lord's.

— Richie Benaud from My Spin on Cricket

OPENER BILL LAWRY LOOKS TO SEE IF THE BALL WILL BE CAUGHT. (BOB THOMAS/GETTY IMAGES)

IAN REDPATH

I first encountered Bill Lawry when I got picked in the Victorian Sheffield Shield squad as a 20-year-old in the summer of 1961–62. The first thing that I learned was that nobody called him Bill. Everyone called him 'the Phantom' or 'Phant' for short. Bill was only four years older than me, but he was already captain of Victoria. He'd been appointed to the office upon his triumphant return home that spring from the 1961 Ashes tour, having played a vital role in Australia's 2–1 series win with two match-winning centuries.

Bill was a hard man. I mean that as a sincere compliment. I witnessed his legendary hardness first-hand when I made my Shield debut for Victoria against South Australia at the MCG in late December 1961. South Australia's captain, Les Favell, won the toss and chose to bat. Bill stationed me in the slips. That's where I fielded for my club, South Melbourne, and where I'd been fielding in Victorian training. We soon had the SACAs 3/94, which brought a very powerful batsman by the name of Neil Dansie to the crease. Neil slashed hard at a wide one and the ball flew off a thickish edge. It burst through my hands and nicked my eyebrow on the way past.

My eyebrow started bleeding. So I approached my captain and said, 'Phant, I got a bit of a nick here'. No pun intended. He took one look at my bleeding eyebrow and swiftly replied, 'Piss off and get it fixed!' There was no 'Are you alright?' or 'How are you feeling?'

I was very fortunate to come into the Victorian side under Bill's leadership. He led by example and the young batsmen such as myself, Bobby Cowper and Keith Stackpole learnt how to succeed as Shield batsmen just by watching him go about his business. He played every game, whether it was for Northcote, Victoria or Australia, as if his life depended on it. At that stage, Shield cricketers weren't professionals, but Bill prepared and behaved like one. He did everything he could to be a successful cricketer. He didn't drink. His after-hours routine during a match consisted of a movie then an early night. He was a very focused cricketer. That certainly showed in his results: he consistently made big runs at all levels.

Bill's a tall man and was very much a front-foot batsman. That helped him in England where the pitches are softer and the ball bounces less. But it posed a bit of a challenge for him when he was playing the short ball on hard, fast Australian pitches. If he couldn't hook or duck a bouncer, Bill's solution was simple: just wear it on the body. He'd often return to the dressing room at the end of the day covered in bruises. He really did play every match as if his life depended on it.

In what turned out to be his antepenultimate Test, Bill played one of the bravest knocks that I've ever seen. We were chasing an improbable 416 for victory on a fourth and fifth day SCG pitch where the ball was going through the top of the pitch. John Snow, a dominant force in that series, wreaked havoc, taking 7/40 off 17.5 overs. We were bowled out for 116 on the final afternoon. Bill finished unbeaten on 60 from 229 balls, one of only two Australian batsmen to reach double digits. It was a magnificent innings.

Off the field, Bill was a down to earth and uncomplicated bloke. He'd come back from the 1961 Ashes tour as a bona fide national hero and that could easily have gone to his head, but he didn't let it. There were never any airs or graces about him. He wasn't a big noter in any respect.

He always mixed in well with the boys. He wasn't aloof. That never changed, even when he became Australian captain in January 1968. And he always had that quirky sense of humour which all of us suffered from at one point or another. His most famous prank – which I didn't witness, but heard about down the grapevine – took place on the 1961 Ashes tour. He and his partner in crime, Frank Misson, a young fast bowler from New South Wales, nailed their captain Richie Benaud's shoes to the floor of the Australian dressing room when he wasn't looking. When Richie put his shoes on, he was glued to the spot! The elimination of those entertaining pranks was the one social change Bill made when he became Australian captain.

As far as hobbies went, his first love was racing pigeons. He also enjoyed fishing and going to the movies. When, years later, I joined him in the Australian team, we often went fishing together when we were on tour. We had some good times fishing outside Durban and up on the Zambezi in Rhodesia.

In my first Shield game, I batted at five. At the beginning of the following season, the summer of 1962–63, I started opening with Bill and we quickly formed a good partnership. I learned how to be a good first-class opener simply by watching him bat from the non-striker's end. Bill looked to constantly rotate the strike and keep the scoreboard ticking over with quick singles. He was a very aggressive runner between the wickets. I loved batting with him.

He was easy to run with because he was a good, loud caller. I can still hear that distinctive, high-pitched nasal voice of his in my head shouting 'yes', 'no' or 'wait'. He was a terrific judge of a run. When it was his call, he backed his own judgement and expected his partner to too. There was never any hesitation. If he said 'no', he meant no.

Apart from his calling, he didn't chat much out in the middle. He diligently went about his business and allowed his partner to do the same. As I said, Bill led by example. He rarely, if ever, told you what to do. He showed you.

I was intensely proud when I returned from England for the start of the 1961–62 season and was appointed Victoria's captain.
— *Bill Lawry*

In Victoria we are a bit one-eyed when it comes to cricket.
— *Bill Lawry*

IAN REDPATH IN 1964.
(NATIONAL ARCHIVES)

KEITH STACKPOLE

I followed the Australian team's progress over the radio once they arrived in England in 1961. In the early tour games, Bill forced his way into the Australian XI for the first Test through his aggressive stroke-play. He was a lovely hooker of the ball and used the shot to good effect. Australia won the Ashes 2–1 and Bill had a wonderful series, topping Australia's run scoring list with 420 Test runs, including hundreds in both of Australia's Test wins, at an average of 52.50. He returned home as an all-conquering Ashes hero and was promptly appointed captain of Victoria.

So, there was a lot expected of Bill when he led his Northcote team to Victoria Park to take on my club, Collingwood, early in the summer of 1961–62. It was Bill's first district club game since his Ashes heroics. In the lead-up to the game, the powers-that-be at our club pulled off something of a transfer coup. They poached a whippy left-arm quick by the name of Charlie Fildes from Melbourne's second XI and installed him in our first XI. When we saw his name in our team sheet on Thursday night, we asked each other, 'Who's this bloke?' None of us knew who he was.

When we arrived at Victoria Park on Saturday morning, Bill won the toss and chose to bat. Our captain, Jack Rose, threw the new ball to Charlie and he soon had the prize wicket of Bill Lawry, trapped LBW for 4. In Northcote's second innings, Charlie did even better, bowling Bill for 2. It was his greatest moment in district cricket!

The next summer – the summer of 1962–63 – I received my first extended run of games in the Victorian Shield team. That's when I started to really get to know Bill. I batted three behind our well-established opening pair of Bill Lawry and Ian Redpath. Bill was quite simply the most passionate Victorian that I've ever known. He loved representing our great state and he spread that love throughout our team. Mind you, I can't recall him ever uttering a single word on the subject. He didn't need to – his actions spoke much louder than his words ever could. There was great rivalry between all the states in those days, but especially between Victoria and New South Wales. By the summer of 1964–65 when I scored my maiden Shield hundred, Bill Lawry and Bobby Simpson had established themselves as one of the world's finest Test opening partnerships. Each of them captained their home state – Victoria and New South Wales respectively – and were great mates, which only heightened the fierce rivalry between Victoria and New South Wales. When the two states faced one another in the Shield, it was virtually Bill versus Simmo, even though there were 10 other people in each team. As a young fella making my way in Shield cricket, they were great matches to play in.

IAN REDPATH

By the middle of my third season of Shield cricket, the partnership between me and Bill was going well. I didn't realise how well until, on Christmas Eve 1963, I got a phone call from a mate informing me that I'd been picked for the second Test against South Africa starting on New Year's Day at the MCG. I was 22 years old. Back then, the Australian selectors didn't call players to tell them that they'd been picked to represent their country. Australian cricketers, like any member of the Australian public, had to listen to the radio for the announcement of the national team. But, because I wasn't expecting to be picked, I wasn't listening to the radio that day.

I was surprised – but delighted – to be picked for the second Test. But I wasn't expecting to play. Three of Australia's stars – captain Richie Benaud and middle-order batsmen Brian Booth and Norm O'Neill – were missing the Test through injury. I thought that Brian and Norm would be replaced on a like-for-like basis by Jack Potter and Barry Shepherd, both of whom were in excellent form for the second Test. The notion of replacing a middle-order batsman with a specialist opener like myself when we already had the world's finest opening partnership in Bob Simpson and Bill Lawry didn't even occur to me.

I got a shock when, on the opening morning of the Test, Bob Simpson, our stand-in captain, came up to me in the nets and said, 'You're opening and I'll be batting down the list.'

It was a wise and team-orientated decision by Simmo. He reasoned that a 22-year-old Test debutant would be more comfortable batting in his usual Shield position

with his usual Shield partner. When I walked out to bat for the first time in Test cricket late on the first evening, it helped having Bill with me. On the last two occasions we'd opened for Victoria, against Queensland and NSW at the MCG, we'd racked up 203 and 140. We made it to stumps that first evening then came back the next day and put on 219 for the first wicket, setting a new record for an Australian Test opening partnership on Australian soil.

That was a wonderful day. It had actually started off with a spot of controversy. Just after the start of play that morning, Joe Partridge, a right-arm fast-medium bowler, dug in a short ball which Bill hooked towards the square-leg fence. A split second later, Bill fell to the ground in front of his stumps and the bails were dislodged. The South Africans – including their captain, Trevor Goddard, who was fielding at gully – quite naturally appealed.

Australian opener Bill Lawry knocked the bails off his wicket when facing South African swing bowler Joe Partridge in the Second Test yesterday. It was the third over of the day and Lawry had not added to his overnight score of four. Lawry made a lofty pull shot off a ball from Partridge. His right foot slipped into his stumps and he fell to the ground. He glanced back at the broken wicket then got up and ran. After the bails fell, Springbok captain Trevor Goddard, wicket-keeper John Waite and other fieldsmen behind the wicket ran in, pointed at the bails and looked expectantly at square-leg umpire Lou Rowan. Umpire Rowan had to decide whether Lawry had completed his shot before his foot hit the wicket. He ruled 'not out' and ran in and replaced the bails.

The South Africans did not seem upset at his decision and went back to their positions quickly. Cricket Law 38 says: 'The striker is out "hit wicket" if, in playing at the ball, he hit down his wicket with his bat or any part of his person.'

— *CANBERRA TIMES*, 2 JANUARY 1964

LAWRY HITS NINE IN CENTURY AT BRISTOL

Australian opening batsman Bill Lawry scored 106 in 227 minutes in the second day of the Australians' match against Gloucester. Lawry reached his 100 in 208 minutes with nine fours at which point the Australians' total was 1/159 in reply to Gloucester's 117. In the previous over he and Redpath had posted the 100 partnership in 131 minutes with Redpath contributing 37. Lawry was out when going for a big hit. He hit nine fours. Despite the handicap of a heavy cold in the head and chest, Lawry followed his 50 and 79 against Worcester with an unbeaten 48 at lunch when Australia had lost 1/73.

RUN OUT

Lawry and Simpson began at a merry clip this morning. Lawry unwound some magnificent shots on both sides of the wicket before he lost Simpson — run out for the second successive innings.

— *CANBERRA TIMES*, 5 MAY 1964

The umpire standing at square leg, a tall Brisbane detective by the name of Lou Rowan, ruled it not out on the basis that Bill had completed his hook shot before setting off for a run whereupon he slipped on the glassy MCG pitch and hit the stumps with his back foot. I thought that Lou made the correct decision, but given how quickly it all happened, I could understand why the South Africans looked a bit miffed and the press called it 'a controversial incident'.

In any event, Bill just stood there calmly waiting for the umpire's decision. Like most Australian cricketers, Bill was not a walker. He believed that he was there to do his job – bat – and the umpire was there to do his. He respected the umpire and accepted every umpire's decision, good or bad. He did not substitute his subjective opinion for that of the men duly empowered to enforce the laws of the game. So dearly did he price his wicket, we used to joke that the Phant would stand and politely wait for the umpire's decision even if all three of his stumps were splayed on the ground!

Once the umpire gave him not out on that second morning at the MCG, Bill just focused on the job at hand and continued on his merry way. By the time he was finally out – caught on the fence hooking, ironically enough – shortly before the close of play, he'd scored 157 off 255 balls. His brisk innings was vital in setting up our eight wicket victory and his strike-rate (61.56) wouldn't look out of place in today's game.

At the end of that summer, I was picked for my first Test tour, the 1964 Ashes. I was 22-years-old and the whole tour was a fantastic experience. We sailed from Perth to Colombo, hopped off the ship to play a one-day game against Ceylon, and then sailed onto Bombay where we jumped on a plane to England.

Upon arriving in England, we soon learned that the English press had labelled us 'the worst team ever to come out of Australia'. It wasn't the first and it wouldn't be the last time that they applied such a label to a touring Australian team.

England had the better of the first two drawn, rain-affected Tests in which Bill and I opened. Simmo made a change for the third Test at Headingley, moving himself from six back up to open with Bill, and shifting me down to three. It was an astute move. We won the Test, taking a 1–0 series lead which we never relinquished, and I played my best Test innings of the tour, an unbeaten 58 off 143 balls in the final innings to help steer us to the target of 109 with seven wickets to spare.

That Test at Headingley was memorable for a host of reasons. Firstly, for the second time that series, Bill and I were involved in an unfortunate mix-up. It was my call and I made a bad one. As a result, he was run-out for 78. I've still got a picture in my mind of him just after the run out, head thrown back in dismay in classic Bill fashion. To this day, I'm sure he thinks I cost him his fourth Test hundred.

I like to joke that I actually helped our team's cause – Bill's dismissal brought Peter Burge to the crease and in a low-scoring Test on a pitch that was doing a bit, the burly Queenslander played a dynamic innings of 160 off 308 balls which won us the match and, as it turned out, the Ashes.

In Australia's first innings of the next Test at Old Trafford, Bill was run out for the third time that series. Fortunately, by that stage, he and Simmo had put on 201 for our first wicket. I had a front row seat to their partnership. It was terrific to watch. It completely took the pressure off the rest of the team and set us up to consolidate the 1–0 series lead that we'd seized in the previous Test. We ended up drawing that fourth Test at Old Trafford and the fifth Test at The Oval to win the series 1–0. Not bad for 'the worst team ever to come out of Australia'!

The Ashes was over, but our Test tour of the northern hemisphere wasn't. We were given about 10 days off in Europe before our flight to the subcontinent left from Rome – where we'd play three Tests against India and one against Pakistan. The Ford Motor Company loaned us four Zephyrs. There were 17 of us, so we divided ourselves four to a car (with one car of five), made our own itineraries and toured Europe for 10 days. It was a fantastic experience. By some miracle, all four cars made it to Rome by the appointed time for our flight to the subcontinent.

BILL LAWRY IN THE NETS AT THE ALBERT GROUND.
(AUSTRALIAN NEWS AND INFORMATION BUREAU/NATIONAL ARCHIVES)

AUSTRALIAN CAPTAIN BOBBY SIMPSON AND BILL LAWRY
WALK TO THE PITCH TO OPEN THE FIRST INNINGS
AGAINST ENGLAND IN MELBOURNE IN 1966. (AUSTRALIAN
NEWS AND INFORMATION BUREAU/D. EDWARDS/NATIONAL LIBRARY
OF AUSTRALIA)

OPENER MAY PASS 2,000 IN THIRD DAY'S PLAY
LAWRY'S MAIN HOPE IN UPHILL FIGHT

Ironman left hander Bill Lawry, poised to top the 2,000-run mark in Test cricket, is Australia's chief batting hope today, the crucial third day of the second Test against the West Indies.

The Australians believe Lawry might play a leading role in blunting the menacing West Indian speed attack of Wesley Hall and Charlie Griffith.

CENTURY STAND WITH SIMPSON

Lawry has figured in century stands with Bob Simpson in the matches against Jamaica and Trinidad this tour, and his most recent innings of 134 not out last week at Queens Park Oval showed he has arrived at his peak. Australian batsmanship has rarely faced such a challenging task as the West Indies team is likely to set it.

— *Canberra Times*, 30 March 1965

LAWRY AND SIMPSON'S PARTNERSHIP MOUNTS

The Australian opening batsmen Bob Simpson and Bill Lawry continued to pile on runs on the second day of the fourth Test against the West Indies today. Resuming at none for 263, they had pushed the score on to 359 at lunch. Simpson was 192 not out with Lawry on 144. Their stand is already an Australian record for the first wicket in all Tests and the best for any wicket for Australia against the West Indies. The Australian pair are within sight of the world record Test opening stand of 413 by the Indians Panjut Roy and Vinoo Mankad against New Zealand in the 1955–56 series.

— *Sydney Morning Herald*, Friday 7 May, 1965

'It was always a great comfort to see Bill at the other end, we knew each other's games backwards and sometimes would look to take a particular end to help each other. I tended to play the spinners a little bit better than Bill. He was a great player of fast bowling and if one or the other was struggling just a little against a particular bowler, you'd take the end where you could best help your mate.
— Bob Simpson

THE FIRST BALL TO OPENER BILL LAWRY IN THE FIRST
TEST IN BRISBANE AGAINST ENGLAND IN 1965. (R. NICOL/
AUSTRALIAN NEWS AND INFORMATION BUREAU/NATIONAL ARCHIVES)

ROLAND PERRY

From Captain Australia

Lawry's best season was 1965–66. He was twenty-eight and at his peak in terms of his ability to concentrate. He hit a record (by any Australian) of 979 runs in eleven innings (seven in the Tests) against Mike Smith's England tourists. They took him 2490 minutes, or a run every 2.5 minutes. He was a key in Australia's struggle to retain the Ashes, but he was not entertaining. The contest against England brought out the best and worst in him. While he couldn't be removed, Australia couldn't be beaten, but the cricket was so tight that it was dull for the average punter. Lawry's efforts epitomised the grim struggles of 1958–59, 1961–63, 1964, 1965–66 and 1968. It wasn't pretty. You had to love Test cricket to enjoy it. Ashes were both the result and prize of wars of attrition from both batsmen and bowlers.

Lawry's scores in the 1965–66 Tests were 166, 88, 78, 0, 33, 119 and 108 – 592 runs in all at 84.57. When he made a duck at Sydney there was palpable relief and even joy from the stoic Poms. Each bowler and fielder imagined a day without facing him. Cowper, Burge and Booth were a pleasure to chase.

Only Victorians could forgive Lawry for his tardiness. Yet serious cricket fans everywhere saw the value in his opening-series knock of 166 at Brisbane. They were with him when he fought back with Simpson in an opening stand of 244 at Adelaide when Australia was one down in the series. In the fifth Test at Melbourne, fans watched or hovered near the TV and radio for his 212-run stand with Cowper, who was en route to immortality with the first (and only) triple century in a Test in Australia.

DISTRICT CRICKET HERO

WAYNE ROBINSON

In the winter of 1961, I was a cricket-loving 17-year-old living 500 metres from Westgarth Street Oval, home of Northcote Cricket Club. Naturally, I decided to try out for Northcote. I was invited to their Annual General Meeting to meet club people. Every person I met at that meeting couldn't stop talking about one thing: a 24-year-old Northcote opener by the name of Bill Lawry who, on his maiden Test tour, was playing a key role in helping Australia win the Ashes.

Thus, I was excited by the prospect of one day playing district cricket for Northcote alongside an actual living, breathing Australian Test cricketer in Bill Lawry.

A little over a year later, on 9 February 1963, I opened with Bill for the very first time. I remember that day well. We were playing Fitzroy at Westgarth Street Oval. I was still only 18 and living at home. My mum knew that I was going to be opening the batting that day with Bill Lawry – Australian Test opener, captain of Victoria and one half of Simpson and Lawry, the greatest opening partnership in the world. So she carefully washed and ironed all my cricket clothes. My white shirt, white pants and white cricket boots were all spotless. She even went to the trouble of starching the collar on my white cricket shirt.

As opening partners, Bill and I went into our home dressing room and sat down next to each other. Bill laid out all his gear – creams, pads, gloves, bat, everything was immaculate – and I carefully took out my gear. Then, he uttered his very first words to me as my opening partner: 'Robbo, where's the rest of your dinner suit?' That was my introduction to Bill's legendary sense of humour!

Opening the batting with Phanto was fantastic for a young first-grader like me. The opposition focused all their attention on getting him out. Meanwhile, I went on my merry way, snicking balls to third man for easy singles. By the time that I started opening with Phanto, his lightning running between the wickets with Bob Simpson was already world famous.

'Listen Robbo,' he said to me, 'don't you worry about it – I'll do the bloody calling.' That suited me just fine. He was a terrific judge of a run and I fully trusted his judgement. In all the times that we batted together, he never got run out. I did get run out a few times – sorry Phanto! – but not much.

Phanto has always been a down-to-earth person. He was, after all, a working plumber well before he was an Australian Test cricketer or Channel 9 commentator. I remember one day, when I was about 17, I was working in a shop as an apprentice electrician and Phanto happened to drive past and see me. He stopped, got out and had a chat with me right there and then.

Off-the-field, he's helped me immensely at two critical

junctures in my career. I started off as an electrician, but wanted to switch careers to become a teacher. Now, in order to do that, I needed a reference. So I asked Phanto.

'Yeah, no worries,' he said. 'I'll do it. You'll have to come up to my place and I'll write it for you.' At the time, he was living in Southernhay Street, Reservoir. So I walked into his place, and he's out back in the pigeon coop, wearing an Australian baggy green cap with pigeon poo all over it!

'Right,' he said, 'we'll go and write the letter.' So, he wrote out the letter and signed it: 'Northcote Cricket Club captain'. As he wrote, he spilled a bit of peanut butter on the letter. He calmly wiped it off and said, 'Aw, that'll look really authentic.'

Once I completed my teacher training, I had to wait to get my posting from the Victorian Ministry of Education. At the time, I was living in Reservoir, so I was hoping to be posted to Broadmeadows. Instead, I was posted to Warrnambool. That wasn't ideal, but I accepted it.

That Thursday night, at Northcote training, I said, 'Listen, Phanto, I'll be playing me last game before Christmas. I've been posted to Warrnambool.'

'You want to go?' he asked.

'Well, no, not really', I said.

'Look,' he said, 'I'm having dinner with Lindsay Thompson tonight.' Thompson was the Victorian Minister for Education.

A day or so later, I got a call from the Ministry of Education. 'I believe you were going to Warrnambool', said the caller. 'We can change your appointment. Wait until you get another phone call from us.'

The day before school started, I got a phone call informing me that I had to go to Treasury Place for a meeting. When I got there, there was a massive queue of around 50 to 60 people. Five minutes later, a voice called out: 'Wayne Robinson'. I walked past everybody in the long queue. They, understandably, didn't look too impressed.

I walked into an office and there was Dick Armitage, the Victorian Director of Education. 'You want to be transferred', he said. 'People like you drive the shit out of me!' Oh, no, I thought to myself. Then, he said: 'Gee, you batted well on Saturday.' It turned out that he was Vice-President of Carlton Cricket Club and a big cricket fan. We talked cricket for the rest of the time and he approved my transfer to Sunshine.

I ended up having a successful career as a teacher, finishing up as an associate director of a university. Phanto helped me get there. That's the kind of bloke that he is – he'll help a mate if he can.

If [I] wasn't hungry for runs and if I ever slipped into an attitude where I didn't really care how many I made, I would rather not play the game. This applies not only to Test matches, but to Shield, pennant and any other matches taken seriously.
— Bill Lawry

TOM RYAN

When I was a kid, cricket was the game for me. Footy and tennis were fun, but cricket had a gravity all its own. My approach to the game was fairly straightforward: an empty garage with the door shut, a tennis ball to hurl against the back wall and a bat to belt the rebound to all four corners of the field or play it sedately back down the pitch. All the while, I'd provide insightful commentary on the sporting miracles I performed, inserting crowd roars or hushed murmurs of approval whenever appropriate. Stylish runs were made, crucial wickets were taken.

My cast of players was made up of batsmen and bowlers from around the world, with Australia primarily represented by some of Victoria's finest. Neil Harvey, Ron Furlong, Jack Potter, Neil Crompton, John Edwards, Ian Meckiff and Lindsay Kline were among them, along with a young left-hander still playing club cricket but bound for glory: Bill Lawry. As far as I was concerned, it seemed like a perfectly logical step for me to join them all in some other kid's dreams somewhere over the rainbow. I'm not sure I actually believed all of this at the time, but my parents took it all in stride.

Cut to no more than five years later. I'd been playing for Riverside, a nurturing club based in Greensborough near where I lived, when the invitation came to try out for Northcote. Northcote! Where Bill Lawry was captain (and where, by the way, one could also rub shoulders with another state player, left-arm wrist-spinner John Wildsmith, a prodigious turner of the ball). The Phantom, or 'Phanta' as I later came to know him, had made his Test debut a couple of years earlier on the 1961 Ashes tour where he'd topped Australia's run scoring list with 420 Test runs, including centuries in each of Australia's Test wins. His average was 52.50 and he'd played a major role in the 2–1 series victory. He was appointed captain of Victoria upon his triumphant return home.

A couple of years passed before I met him. He spent more than half his time away from the club, playing Tests and state matches, so he was only an occasional presence at the Westgarth Street ground. But whenever he turned up, he brought with him an aura that ensured that we were all on our best behaviour. I used to watch him batting in the practice nets, or bowling his left-arm loops, but, since the senior players and the juniors generally didn't mix (unless you'd become a contender for promotion), I never got to try out my version of off-spin on him or face his imitations of a bowler.

I made my debut in the Northcote firsts in late November 1965 against Hawthorn-East Melbourne at Glenferrie Oval, batting in the middle-order. I was 19, studying to become a teacher and about to begin an Arts course at Monash University. The Phantom was only available for the first day, his higher responsibilities summoning him elsewhere on the second. He shook my

MEMBERS OF THE HAWTHORN-EAST MELBOURNE CRICKET
TEAM RAISE THE PREMIERSHIP FLAG BEFORE THE START
OF THE 1963–64 DISTRICT CRICKET SEASON. BILL LAWRY,
CAPTAIN OF THE NORTHCOTE TEAM, STANDS AT THE LEFT.
(FAIRFAX)

hand and wished me luck in the dressing room, then lost the toss – there's no connection whatsoever between those two events – and we were sent in on a sticky wicket. He made five runs, five times my contribution at number seven. We batted one short in the second innings because of his absence, but still somehow managed to win, largely because of left-arm medium-pacer Ken Walker's ability to exploit the conditions. For the match, he took 11/27 off 22 overs. Unbelievably, he never played for Victoria.

Phanta was elsewhere for the next seven games and the next time we saw him was our final home-and-away match of the season. We were playing University, an away game that we had to win in order to make the finals. Thanks to the patient selectors, I was still in the team. We had the Phantom back, but they had the magisterial 19-year-old Paul Sheahan, who'd made his Shield debut for Victoria 11 weeks earlier and was less than two years away from his Test debut. On day one, they only made 153 on a decent batting track, with Sheahan contributing 20. At stumps we were 1/37 and feeling confident, with our leader 17 not out. But on day two, things began to fall apart, especially after Phanta was run out for 46.

When I say he was run out, I should add that I was the other batsman at the time. I'd just arrived at the crease and, despite his reassurances, wasn't playing with much confidence. I turned the ball ten metres or so past short leg and he yelled 'yes' as he charged down the pitch to try to get me off strike. I should have said 'no', but who am I to say 'no' to Bill Lawry, and he was left well short of the crease. Then I was given out LBW shortly afterwards. It took a defiant 20 run ninth wicket partnership between wicket-keeper Barry Morrison and fast bowler Mike Mitton to get us over the line.

As a result, we made it into the finals.

The two key matches in that premiership-winning season were the semi-final against Richmond and our final regular season game against University. We had to win the game against University to claim the fourth and last place in the finals.

The match went right down to the wire. We were chasing 154 for victory and were eight down for about 150. A catch went up in the air and a University player by the name of Tony Steele, a friend of mine, didn't go for it. University were out of finals contention and we've always suspected that Tony chose to help us out by not going for the catch. He's always denied it of course, because he has to, but we Northcote lads have had a good chuckle about it over the years.

— Wayne Robinson

BARRY MORRISON

He's always been a very level-headed bloke. His mood doesn't go up and down. It stays nice and constant. So, when he returned home from the 1961 Ashes tour as an all-conquering hero, having topped Australia's tour run scoring list with 2019 first-class runs at an average of 61.18 and 420 Test runs, including two match-winning Test hundreds, at an average of 52.50 to help Australia win the Ashes 2–1, he didn't change at all. He was the same old Phantom with perhaps a few more attacking strokes. That being said, he was still very hard to get out!

Fast-forward four years to the summer of 1965–66. By that stage, the 28-year-old Phantom had established himself as one of the finest openers in the world. At the conclusion of Australia's final Test of the summer, against England at the MCG, he'd played 35 Tests and scored 2876 runs, including eight hundreds, at an average of 50.45. Australia drew that Test and the five match home Ashes series 1–1 to retain the Ashes that they'd won in England in 1964, but there was still one major cricketing prize that Bill could win that summer: Melbourne's district club competition, which Northcote hadn't won in 54 years.

We had to win our final regular season game, against University at University, just to make the finals. The match was played on the Saturday and the Monday of Labour Day weekend. When we turned up on Saturday morning, it was a good batting strip. Now, in those days, in order to get the win, you had to get all 10 wickets. A team batting second could force a draw even though it had scored less runs than the team batting first, if it did not lose all 10 of its wickets. Therefore, upon winning the toss, Bill decided to send University in, as we had to win the game to make the finals.

We rolled them for 153 then reached 1/37 at the close of play. Crucially, the Phantom remained unbeaten on 17 and we looked forward to batting on Monday after the pitch had had a day to dry out. Unfortunately, it rained on Sunday and the pitch was still a bit wet when we turned up the next day. We were going ok until, disastrously, the Phantom got run out – I can't remember how – for 46. Things plummeted alarmingly from there. (Our middle order batting wasn't exactly our strength.) By the time that our number 10, Michael Mitton, joined me at the crease, we still needed 18 runs to win.

According to my mum, the Phantom looked pretty nervous at that point. As the partnership between

We were bowled out for 82 in 22.5 overs and 110 minutes. You could see the divots in the pitch where every ball landed. After landing, the ball could go anywhere: it could just as easily leap over your head as shoot low into your shoelaces.

Phanto wasn't down and neither were we. 'Look,' he said, 'if we can get into these guys early, we're a big chance.' We believed that we were in the game. That pitch was still diabolical and we had the best medium-pace swing bowler in the competition in Kenny Walker.

Kenny ripped through the Richmond batting order. He was swinging the ball a metre both ways. He was unplayable. At one stage, he had 5/1. When rain stopped play at 4:39pm, Richmond were 6/18 and Kenny had the figures of 6/4 – that's not a typo – from five overs.

After play that evening, we all went to the bar for a drink. Phanto, being a teetotaller, had a lemon squash.
— Wayne Robinson

Michael and myself grew, he told everyone not to move from their seats. (We cricketers are a superstitious bunch.) The only problem was that the Phantom himself was so nervous that he couldn't follow his own rule – he paced around the pavilion, willing us over the line. Somehow, Michael and I got the 18 runs we needed to defeat University and Bill finally stopped pacing.

A week later, we took on Richmond in the semi-final at Punt Road. Because it was a semi-final, the pitch was covered. Unfortunately, the covers leaked and it was very wet at one end when we turned up on Saturday morning. Richmond's captain, Dave Cowper, Bob's older brother, won the toss and sent us in. 'Well,' said Bill when he got back from the toss, 'that was bad luck. We've got to get out of this the best way we can.'

One end of the track was wet and batting was difficult to say the least. Richmond had an excellent paceman by the name of Graeme Paterson. Patto was the first bowler I ever faced who was able to bowl what we now call reverse swing. He was just about unplayable that morning, bowling into the wet end. Only two of us – the Phantom and myself – reached double figures. I got 21 and the Phantom top scored with 32. It would turn out to be the most valuable 32 that he ever scored. After 22.5 overs, we were bowled out for 82.

Fortunately, one end of the pitch was still wet and Kenny Walker, a little left-arm seamer, ripped through Richmond's batting line-up. At the close of play on the first day, Richmond were 6/18 and Kenny had taken all six of Richmond's wickets to fall. He came back the next Saturday and completed the job, finishing with 9/28 – the other Richmond wicket which fell was a run-out – to roll Richmond for 60 to give us a 22 run first innings lead.

Given that 20 wickets had fallen in one and a half days, Richmond would've harboured hopes of a second innings turnaround and an outright win. The Phantom snuffed that out with an opening stand of 179 with Wayne 'Groucho' Robinson.

BARRY MORRISON

The Grand Final against Essendon would be played at the Albert Ground a week later. In the week leading up to the Grand Final, we were able to practise together as a team at the ground. That was helpful. We all knew that our middle order batting was our weakness. The Phantom came up with clear plans for what we would do if certain scenarios arose and assigned the nightwatchman's duties to me. We went in with an unchanged side. We knew that we were underdogs by a long shot.

Essendon had three players – all-rounder John Swanson, right-arm fast-medium bowler John Grant and leg-spinner Keith Kirby, who'd played first-class cricket for Victoria, as well as Daryl Foster, who'd played for the Victorian Second XI and would go on to coach Western Australia to nine Sheffield Shields. We just had the Phantom. Man for man, Essendon were clearly the stronger side. Our strength was that we gelled well together as a team and everyone knew what their role was. Nobody ever had to be told what to do.

The opening day of the Grand Final didn't quite go to plan. Essendon's captain, Ian Monks, won the toss and chose to bat. By the end of the day, they were 6/311. We just could not get them out. With the exception of their opener, Raymond Howe, all of their batsmen reached 20. They hit us everywhere.

Nothing went our way. When he was on about 30, their other opener, Monksy, nicked a ball from Michael Mitton and I took the routine catch behind the stumps. We all appealed. The umpire was none other than Bill Smyth, the best umpire in Victoria, if not Australia. He gave it not out. We couldn't believe it. Groucho, standing next to me at first slip, went berserk. I looked at the Phantom, standing in his usual position at cover, and he looked at me. Then, we just got on with it – as did Monksy, who went on to make 136!

As we approached tea on day two, things were not looking good. Essendon's numbers seven, eight, nine and 10 batsmen had all reached 50, taking their team total past 500. In an act of sheer desperation, the Phantom brought himself on to bowl his left-arm orthodox spin for an over. As the wicket-keeper, I distinctly remember him bowling to a right-handed batsman. He bowled a wide down the leg-side that was so wide, it landed off the pitch and went for four byes. That was the first and only time I saw the Phantom bowl in a match.

Essendon declared at 9/514 at tea on day two. At tea, the Phantom had a brief chat with our team that has become legendary. Everyone present recalls the precise words that he used slightly differently, but this is what I remember him saying: 'Someone bat with me and we'll make them. Someone's got to stay with me.'

BILL LAWRY, CAPTAIN OF NORTHCOTE, ENTERS THE GROUND
WITH TOM RYAN IN THE DISTRICT FINAL. (PROVIDED BY TOM RYAN)

THE WINNING NORTHCOTE TEAM.
(PROVIDED BY TOM RYAN)

At the close of play that day, we were 0/98 chasing 515 with the Phantom unbeaten on 53 and Groucho unbeaten on 33. As the designated nightwatchman, I'd watched the action closely with my pads on. John Grant, a pint-sized, nippy right-arm fast-medium bowler who went on to play 43 first-class matches for Victoria, bowled well that evening, beating the Phantom on a few occasions and getting him to nick one that their keeper Tommy O'Neill couldn't quite grasp. But the Phantom didn't let that bother him. One of his great strengths is his ability to forget the last ball and focus on the next one. He maintains a positive mindset. By contrast, club batsmen like myself tend to fall into negative thinking: 'Aw, I've been beaten twice this over. What's going to happen this next ball?'

At the end of that day, I was cautiously optimistic. We were in the game, but 515 is a lot of runs and we still had to start well the next morning. Day three was when things really turned in our favour. Bill was tremendous, scoring fluently throughout the course of the entire day. The problem was that we kept losing wickets at reasonably regular intervals. We lost our first wicket at 130, our second at 206 and our third at 219.

At that point, the game was in the balance. A few quick wickets and victory would be within Essendon's reach. The 21-year-old Tommy Ryan walked to the crease. He was a university student in his maiden season of first grade. In his entire life, he'd only scored 96 first-grade runs. Tommy played the innings of his life and his partnership with the Phantom just grew and grew. Late in the day, our total neared 400 and we were still only three wickets down. That's when I thought, hang on, we're a genuine chance here. At the close of play on day three, we were 3/405 with the Phantom unbeaten on 236 and Tommy unbeaten on 77.

The match was by no means won. As long as the Phantom stayed there, I thought that we were in a good position, but if Essendon could somehow remove the Phantom, they'd be favourites again. By the start of day four, word had clearly gotten out about our miraculous run chase. The Albert Ground, which only holds about 4000 or 5000 people, was full. Nobody could get in.

Tommy fell early for 82 and we needed 104 to win with six wickets in hand. Frank Brew, a left-arm wrist-spinner, walked out to join the Phantom. Brewy wasn't a proper number six batsman, but he was an aggressive hitter. His approach was perfect for the match situation. With the Phantom batting fluently at one end, Brewy smashed a quick-fire 47 to kill off the game.

Shortly before 2pm, the Phantom hit the winning runs. He finished unbeaten on 282 as we won by five wickets with half a day to spare. To this day, he tells me that that knock was one of the two best he played in his life, the other being his match-winning maiden Test century at the 'Battle of the Ridge' at Lord's in 1961.

I do not seek 100s and 200s because they will merely boost my aggregates and averages, but rather because these are the scores that win matches. The breezy 30s and 40s may be easy on the eye for spectators but show me the matches that they win.
— Bill Lawry

In 2000, the Victorian Cricket Umpires Association voted the District final 'the District match of the century'.

It was different, I suppose. We were playing as amateurs. We just went out to enjoy batting. I just enjoyed batting. I think today, obviously, you are getting a lot of money to perform well. We probably had a different attitude. We just played to win the game.

— Bill Lawry

Test opener and Victorian captain Bill Lawry scored 282 for Northcote in leading it to victory in the Melbourne district cricket final yesterday. Essendon had appeared certain of victory when it scored 514 for the loss of nine wickets in its first innings. However, Northcote still had five wickets in hand when Lawry hooked for four runs to boost his side's total to 516. Northcote batted for 509 minutes to score 5/516 off 122.1 overs. Essendon batted two minutes less for 514 runs, and faced one ball less. Thus, when each had faced the same number of balls, the scores were level, and Lawry scored the winning runs off the first ball of the 123rd over. Lawry's inning's took 509 minutes with 32 fours. It was a determined and polished display, with rarely a false stroke, and it took his pennant aggregate to 714 runs in 10 innings, with four times not out, his average was 119. As he had made 1,445 runs in first-class games during the season he thus had the splendid figures of 2,159 for an average of 83. His 282 not out was the highest ever in a final, and was next best to Bill Ponsford's 295, made in a semi-final.

— *Canberra Times*, 18 April 1966

BILL LAWRY HAS A CLOSE CALL AT 205 RUNS IN THE DISTRICT FINAL AGAINST ESSENDON. (FAIRFAX)

WAYNE ROBINSON

When Lawry went long

I opened the batting with Bill Lawry when he scored 282 not out for Northcote against Essendon to win the 1965–66 Victoria Cricket Association Premiership final.

I was a 22-year-old in my fourth year of grade cricket. Bill had just come off a hundred at the MCG against England that helped Australia retain the Ashes.

He batted for 509 minutes and faced 454 balls. It was a two innings match, supposed to be played over two weekends. But the rules were that if there was no chance of getting both innings in, the match would be decided on whoever scored the most runs in their first innings. The first innings had to be played to a finish, though.

It took three weekends to finish this game. Essendon scored 514 for 9 declared, batting first. That's a lot of runs, someone said in our dressing room, after we'd come off. Bill didn't think it was enough, though. The wicket was good and he couldn't understand why they'd declared. 'This is a Grand Final,' he told everyone.

Earlier in the season, he had made a duck against Essendon. He's got a memory like an elephant, forgets nothing, and was determined to make up for this rare failure. Straightaway he started accumulating runs. Nothing flash, just like he was playing in a Test match.

That's what stood out about Bill. He played club cricket just as seriously and carefully as if he was playing for Australia.

I was dropped at third slip first ball, but was still there at the close of play. We had 98 by then. Bill said that if

I didn't get out in the first hour the next day, we'd win the game. He also told me not to play back to their leg-spinner. The next day, just after the hour, I played back to the leg-spinner and was out lbw.

Bill didn't give a single chance in his 282, in almost two and a half days of batting. It was the same whenever he batted. Never looked like getting out.

Bill saw the ball much earlier than the rest of us, and at club level didn't appear to have any weaknesses. He judged the ball perfectly outside off stump. Even when the opposition had their state players, Bill dominated, simply by having complete mastery of his game.

Playing with someone that good inspired you to play better yourself. Our middle-order batsman Tom Ryan was a bit of a hitter, but for the final, Bill just said to him. 'Cut that out today.' Tom scored 82 and put on nearly 200 with Bill.

As a captain, Bill was a hard taskmaster, but people listened to him. He dropped me to no. 11 for one game because I questioned one of his decisions.

The final against Essendon was played at the Albert Ground in Melbourne, the Melbourne Cricket Club's second ground. I'd never seen it so full. As Bill closed in on the target, there was a 70-metre queue outside to get in.

NORTHCOTE SKIPPER BILL LAWRY (CENTRE) CELEBRATES
VICTORY WITH TEAMMATES (CLOCKWISE) TOM RYAN,
BOB GOSSTRAY, BARRY MORRISON,
KEN WALKER AND FRANK BREW. (FAIRFAX)

TOM RYAN

The Albert Ground was a picture of serenity when we arrived there for the Grand Final. A mirage-like, village green idyll off St Kilda Road in the heart of inner-suburban Melbourne, it provided the perfect setting for what the Phantom was to look back on, half a century later, as 'one of the greatest experiences of my life'.

We were the underdogs. Essendon had the best attack in the competition and a strong batting line up. All we had to do, we thought, was keep them to a reasonably low score and we had a chance. The pitch was a batting paradise. Essendon captain Ian Monks won the toss and, unsurprisingly, chose to bat. Our opponents ended the first day on 6/311. Monks made a sterling 136 and our 17-year-old second change bowler, Paul Shanahan, finished with a creditable 3/88 off 24 overs.

I took 1/31 off 10 very mediocre overs of pseudo off-spin. An exasperated Phanta threw me the ball late in the day, pointed to a spot on the pitch and told me to bowl at it when Monks was on strike. I did and Monks, apparently as unaware of the devious strategy being deployed against him as I was, clubbed the ball straight back at me. In a flash, the Phantom, who'd stationed himself at short mid-off, reached across in front of me and snaffled it.

Monks declared at 9/514 at tea on day two. Phanta thought he was crazy to do so: there were still more runs to be made. But it wouldn't have mattered how many Essendon had made: they were destined to lose. Between innings, there was a surprising air of optimism in our dressing room. Phanta didn't say much, but there was a look on his face that suggested he had something to prove. Perhaps his determination stemmed from a tussle with Essendon earlier in the season when he'd been

dismissed for a duck, Monks' men hollering in delight as he departed. Fast bowler John Grant later recalled him coming to the Essendon dressing room after the day's play and saying, 'You bastards are going to pay for that'.

We ended the first day of the Grand Final 0/98, with Phanta on 53 and Wayne Robinson on 33. At that point, the match suddenly became news in Melbourne. A crowd of a few thousand turned up the following Monday. I was batting at number five. By the time our third wicket fell, we'd advanced to 219, less than halfway to our victory target of 515. Bill was on 130-odd. When I arrived at the crease, he said, 'Don't watch the scoreboard: play the game ball-by-ball and let the score build that way'. It was perhaps the best batting advice that I ever received. He also gave me some more specific guidance about how to handle Essendon's excellent attack: 'If you insist on trying to hook Granty, be careful of the fieldsman at deep backward square. If you're not reading Kirby's wrong'un, play him from the crease.' I wasn't, I did and it worked. Phanta also mentioned something about 'no risky runs', which was the first – and last – time he alluded to our unfortunate mix-up against University a month earlier.

By the time that stumps were drawn on day three, shortly after Essendon had taken the second new ball, we were 3/405. Phanta was 236 not out and I was 77 not out. In the space of a single day, he had almost single-

BILL LAWRY IN 2001 IN FRONT
OF THE SCOREBOARD AT THE
NORTHCOTE CRICKET OVAL
NOW CALLED BILL LAWRY OVAL.
(NEWS LTD/NEWSPIX)

handedly turned a certain defeat into a probable win.

Day four of the game came, along with the first week of the football season. The decent crowd from the previous day had almost tripled in size and the ground was packed. Those who couldn't squeeze inside parked around the perimeter of the ground and stood on their cars to peer over the fence. I lasted only a few minutes, but then 39-year-old Frank Brew, a Northcote legend, joined Phanta out in the middle and belted 47 from 56 balls to put the game beyond doubt. Fittingly, Phanta hit the winning runs, finishing on 282 not out, the highest score in a District final since Bill Ponsford made 295 for St Kilda in 1927. His innings and that match are now part of Australian cricket folklore.

Bill Lawry led Australia to the top of Test cricket in the late 1960s. He ranks, along with fellow left-hander Arthur Morris, as well as Bob Simpson and Bill Ponsford, as one of the top openers Australia produced in the twentieth century.
— Roland Perry

CAPTAIN

BILL LAWRY AT THE START OF THE
1968 TOUR OF ENGLAND. (PATRICK
EAGER/POPPERFOTO/GETTY IMAGES)

RICHIE BENAUD

From *Willow Patterns*

Lawry is something of an anonymous character to many cricket followers and yet I believe that by the time he has finished he will have carved his own niche in Australian cricket. Certainly on the England tour in 1968 he began the right way by inspiring his team to an against-the odds-victory at Old Trafford over a side that had recently beaten the West Indies in the Caribbean. The Australian team had no right to win this game for they had played in moderate fashion up to the first Test and I am certain Lawry himself would have been content with a draw. But the real test of captaincy is the ability to inspire a team and, in this case, I firmly believe it was Lawry's inspiration, as well as the underlying ability of the young players, that so shocked England.

Four cricket captains. Sir Donald Bradman, Richie Benaud, Bill Lawry and Nawab of Pataudi, in 1968. (Fairfax)

SIMPSON QUITS AS CRICKET LEADER; LAWRY NEXT?

Australian Test captain Bobby Simpson will retire from first-class cricket at the end of this season, and will write for a London newspaper during the Australian tour of England next year.

Simpson today notified the secretary of the Australian Cricket Board of Control, Mr Allan Barnes, of his impending retirement.

— *Canberra Times*, 6 January 1968

BILL LAWRY VICTORIA'S TEST CAPTAINCY HOPE

Bill Lawry, Bobby Simpson's opening partner, who seems certain to lead Australia in the remaining two Tests against India and to England next year, would be the first Victorian to captain Australia since 1956. Since then, Australia has been captained by Richie Benaud and Simpson, both serving record terms in numbers of Tests. Simpson says he would not retire if he did not have a great admiration for Lawry, whom he says, will make a good captain.

Lawry and Simpson have proved themselves perhaps the most reliable opening partnership Australia has had for years. Two of their stands are the highest against England, and with three other century opening partnerships they have scored two more than any other pair against England. They also scored the best stand against the West Indies, 382, when each scored a double century.

LAWRY TOUR CAPTAIN

The Victorian captain, Bill Lawry, will lead Australia's defence of the Ashes when the Australian cricket team tours England this year.

The confirmation of Lawry's appointment came from the Australian Cricket Board of Control in Sydney yesterday.

— Bill Phippard, *Canberra Times*, 1 March 1968

THE AUSTRALIAN TEAM IS
WELCOMED BY THE PRESS
IN ENGLAND IN 1968.
(DENNIS OULDS/CENTRAL PRESS/
HUTTON ARCHIVE/GETTY IMAGES)

IAN REDPATH

Nearly three-and-a-half years later, in mid-January 1968, Bill succeeded Simmo as Australian Test captain. He didn't change at all as a bloke. He was still the same old Bill. Even before they put the 'C' in front of his name, he'd long been a senior batsman and a leader by example.

He inherited a team that was in a rebuilding phase. We'd lost three fine Test batsmen in Simpson, Burge and Booth. That left Bill as our best and most experienced Test batsman. As a result, his batting became a bit more circumspect.

From his very first Test as captain, Bill stood up to the Australian Board of Control for International Cricket – which would change its name to the Australian Cricket Board in 1973 and to Cricket Australia in 2003 – for his players' rights. We were playing India up at the Gabba. It was over 40 degrees and humid when we arrived in Brisbane to discover that, instead of staying at our usual hotel – Lennons – in the city, we were staying in a motel out in the suburbs. The rooms were tiny and all we had for cooling were some ceiling fans which circulated slowly over our heads. We weren't happy.

About 20 minutes after we put our bags in our rooms, Bill got us all together and announced, 'Right-o fellas, pick up your bags, we're going to Lennons'. I think he might've rung Lennons himself to make our booking! The original booking at the motel in the suburbs had been made by the Queensland Cricket Association's delegates to the Board. Bill wasn't too popular with them

after that. He did the right thing by his players, but, in so doing, he undermined himself politically with the Board which had appointed him.

A year into his captaincy, Bill made a decision that saved my Test career. Leading into the third Test against the West Indies at the SCG in early January 1969, I'd been in a slump, averaging 25.76 in my last seven Tests and passing fifty just thrice. I was worried that I was going to be dropped. As we were coming off the ground on the second morning after bowling the West Indies out for 264, Bill walked up to me and said, 'I'm going to make a change. I want you to bat down the list and I'll open with Stack [Keith Stackpole]'.

It was a left-field move. Bill and I had been opening together for Victoria and Australia for years. Stack always came in at three for Victoria. He didn't even open for his club, Collingwood, for whom he generally batted at three or four. Bill's gambit paid off immediately. Stack got 58 off 80 balls and put on an opening partnership of 68 with Bill. I got 80 off 132 balls batting at four. After that, Stack became an excellent Test opener for Australia, averaging 40.50 in 33 Tests in that position, and I had two productive years in the middle order, averaging 46.39 in 18 Tests.

Colin Cowdrey wins the toss before the Third Test at Edgbaston in July 1968.
(STAFF/MIRRORPIX/GETTY IMAGES)

BILL LAWRY LEADING THE TEAM ONTO
THE GROUND DURING THE FOURTH TEST
IN 1968. (NEWSPIX)

ROLAND PERRY

From *Captain Australia*

In his first Test as captain, at Brisbane during the 1967–68 series versus India, Bill Lawry did everything right. He launched Australia's innings with 64 and 45 in partnerships with Ian Redpath of 76 and 116. When India batted, he juggled his unpenetrating attack with intelligence and got the best out of them. Yet still Lawry received plenty of abuse from the Brisbane crowd.

There was some prejudice against Bill Lawry brought on by a decade of watching him bat. Lawry, the left-hander, could attack when he liked. He was a powerful, gutsy hooker. A familiar sight was seeing the hunch-backed, tight-shoulder shot as he swivelled through it. He had the traditional left-hander's penchant for the on side, but usually in first-class cricket he had plundered it more slowly and monotonously than the average punter could stomach, especially as Lawry's powers of concentration allowed him to be around for a long time – sometimes a day or two. He saw his job as pushing Australia or Victoria off to a good start. More often than not he defended his way forward. It was Bill's way and he was steadfast.

He also accepted the abuse. It was a lot less painful than a ball in the chest from Fred Trueman, or one on the shoulder from Charlie Griffith. Once, when a predecessor, Jim Burke, was heckled at Melbourne, he offered his bat to the abuser. It was Lawry's sentiment too but he would never have reacted with such a gesture. Lawry would simply pretend he didn't hear a negative comment. Or maybe he didn't. Few had his concentration at the wicket. It resembled a trance at times, especially when he had

decided to up the shutters, see an opposing bowler off or bat through an innings, which he did five times.

In his first match at the helm he was accused of giving his fellow Victorians more than their share of the bowling. 'Hey Lawry,' someone called. 'Give Gleeson a bowl – his grandmother lives in Geelong.' After New South Wales paceman Dave Renneberg had warmed up for three overs, another spectator yelled, 'Hey Renneberg, just tell Lawry you were born in Victoria'. The bowling figures showed that Lawry didn't favour his fellow state players. The two Victorians, Bob Cowper and Alan Connolly, sent down 87.6 overs. The other four non-Victorians, Ian Chappell (South Australia), Dave Renneberg (New South Wales), John Gleeson (New South Wales) and Eric Freeman (South Australia) sent down 122. But Lawry did give Cowper the longest spells in the last innings of the match when the ball was turning. In India's first innings Cowper had the best figures, with three for 31 off fifteen. Sensing Cowper was 'hot', Lawry asked him to send down 39.6 in India's second dig. Cowper took four for 104, making the important breakthroughs to dismiss M. L. Jaisimha (101) and C. G. Borde (63). It was a matter of judgment.

THE AUSTRALIAN CRICKET TEAM DURING THEIR TOUR OF ENGLAND. BACK ROW (LEFT-RIGHT): LES JOSLIN, JOHN INVERARITY, BILL LAWRY (CAPTAIN), PAUL SHEAHAN, DAVID RENNEBERG, NEIL HAWKE, IAN REDPATH. FRONT ROW: BOB COWPER, BRIAN TABER, DOUG WALTERS, JOHN GLEESON. (PHOTO BY BOB THOMAS/GETTY IMAGES)

Lawry put his faith in the 'Wallaby' Cowper and his off spin. Australia won by 39 runs.

In the final Test of the series – the fourth at the Sydney Cricket Ground – the scenario was much the same. Lawry scored 66 and 52 in opening stands, this time with Cowper, of 61 and 111. In the fourth Test India chased 395 to win. In the fifth, it was 342. This time Lawry had Bob Simpson, the skipper he had replaced, bowl leg spin. It gave the attack a balanced spin combination. Even the Indians, fed on spin soon after birth, could not cope on a Sydney turner. Simpson took five for 59, Cowper four for 49. Australia won this time by 144 runs.

Now captain, it was a sure bet that Lawry would be even more intent on defending his wicket. He felt the responsibility and was determined not to fail as a batsman while skipper, or let Australia be beaten. In the 1968 Ashes, he began with an astonishing burst of scoring after lunch on day one in the first Test at Old Trafford. He attacked off-spinner Pat Pocock with 2 sixes and 6 fours in his 81 that set his team on the way. Inspired, Doug Walters (81), Paul Sheahan (88) and Ian Chappell (73 run out) took Australia to four for 319 at stumps. Australia was all out for 357 on the morning of day two, but this enterprise took England by surprise. The tourists won by 159 runs and moved one up.

Rain cut the Lord's Test in half and guaranteed a draw. Lawry's finger was broken in the third Test at Edgbaston, and on 6 he retired hurt but not humiliated. The game was drawn. Rain again reduced play by a day.

Lawry missed the fourth Test at Leeds, when Barry

Jarman led the Australians. But it was Lawry, in the dressing room, who took the flak for the decision to defend for a draw to retain the Ashes rather than go for a win.

Lawry's 135 at The Oval in the fifth Test took him 450 minutes and earned him the sobriquet 'the corpse with pads' from English journalist Ian Wooldridge. Yet it was the only century by an Australian in the series. He stood between England and victory. When corpulent Colin Milburn caught him off 'Big Dave' Brown for 4 in the second innings, John Woodcock noted: 'If the English side could have thrown Milburn aloft they would have.' He added, 'Lawry is a great battler and a wonderfully sound judge of length. All too often he has been the rock on which England foundered.'

The series that began so boisterously for Lawry and his team ended one all. But the skipper was not crestfallen. He had defended the Ashes. They were still retained by Australia.

Lawry emerged as a relentless skipper. He berated his bowlers if they didn't perform and was uncompromising in his attitude to opposing batsmen, not even allowing a drink for a thirsty foe other than at the normal breaks. Yet his way was effective in producing wins for Australia.

Lawry had further success in India, winning three-one under the most testing conditions yet endured by Australians abroad. In Bombay during the First Test, the crowd rioted after a caught-behind decision riled them. Thick smoke engulfed the ground. Bottles were thrown. People began to push on a fence that looked likely to collapse. Ian Chappell urged his skipper to group the players at the end of play so that they could leave the field as a united squad. Lawry didn't seem to hear. 'Hell,' he said, 'we need a wicket badly.'

The captain got his wicket. India was all out in the second innings for 137, leaving Australia just 64 to win. It lost two wickets reaching them before another riot.

More than once the Australians were pelted with stones on the tour. Six people were killed while queuing for tickets to the Test in Calcutta.

It set a sad tone that deteriorated into abuse on the final day as Australia chased just 42 to win. Fans threw bottles and rubbish from the stands. The mess had to be cleaned up and there was a threat of worse action. But Lawry was not leaving the centre until he and Keith Stackpole picked off the runs.

During the break, Lawry used his bat to prod an Indian photographer who had run onto the ground. Australia secured the runs and the opprobrium of the media. They wore black armbands in protest at the tourists' next match. It prompted the media in general to increase their criticism of the Australian skipper. The media had been biased; now it turned nasty. It incited crowd behavior rather than attempting to placate it. Media reaction reached absurd proportions after Lawry pulled away from the wicket when a woman in a sari sat in front of the sightscreen at Bangalore. He was accused of insulting Indian womanhood.

I believe the captaincy will be the making of him.
— Richie Benaud

I think back, and I think I have been very lucky. The fact that I played and toured England for seven months, and played every county, and did it for no money, gave me more of an appreciation of the game. The difference was, when I played, you never said you had an injury, because if you dropped off, you never got back. Players get injured today, they put them on leave for months, and back they come.
— Bill Lawry

GREG CHAPPELL

I got the opportunity to properly watch Bill Lawry bat in a Test match for the first time when I was 20 and in England playing my first season of county cricket with Somerset. Australia was in England that summer for a five Test Ashes series. Bill had by then established himself as one of the finest opening batsmen in the world and seven months earlier, he'd been appointed Australia's 32nd Test captain. Australia's 1968 Ashes tour of England was his first major assignment.

Heading into the final Test at The Oval, Australia held the Ashes and a 1–0 series lead. I bought myself a ticket in the members' area and sat directly behind the slips for a right-handed batsman and leg-slip for a left-handed batsman like Bill. Australia finished day three on 7/264, still 230 runs in arrears of England's mammoth first innings total of 494. Ashley Mallett was unbeaten on 7 and Bill was unbeaten on 135.

By that stage, the young dasher who I'd heard put England to the sword in 1961 was gone. In his place was a different kind of batsman, a huge accumulator of runs who'd eschewed a number of attacking shots in order to minimise risk. Still, there was much to admire in his batting: he was stoic, determined, gritty and very strong-willed. Once he set his mind to do something with the bat, he generally did it.

That hundred that he got at The Oval in '68 was one of the most courageous that I've ever seen. The entire third day was just Bill versus England. He had decided that he wasn't getting out and they didn't look like getting him out. Early the next morning, Bill tried to glance a ball from John Snow down the leg-side. Sitting directly behind where leg-slip would've been, I had the perfect view: Bill missed the ball and it brushed his thigh pad on its way through to the keeper, Alan Knott. England appealed and the umpire gave it out. I remember Bill looking disappointed – that was about as much emotion as I ever saw out of him in his playing days – as he turned to walk back to the pavilion. It was a crucial moment in the Test match and Bill knew it. We were promptly bowled out for 324 in our first innings, handing England a 170 run first innings lead which they duly converted into a comfortable 226 run victory.

LAWRY'S SIGHTS ON THIRD TEST

Australian cricket captain Bill Lawry today outlined a policy of all-out aggression for the third Test against England, starting at Edgbaston on Thursday.

Lawry said it would be fatal for Australia to try to sit on its 1–0 lead in the series. 'We have got to forget we are one-up in this rubber', he said. 'We have just got to start from scratch. At Manchester we went into the first Test with nothing to lose. Nobody thought we would win it but ourselves. Since then we have had the bad period that seems to affect every tourist team at some stage. We were beaten by Yorkshire, the best county in England, and we managed to struggle through the Lord's Test, so we have had this slump at the best time. It would be fatal in the three remaining Tests for us just to try to hold on to our lead because we are not a good enough side for that. Our policy will be to go all out to win the next three Tests'. England's policy is all out aggression too, judged by the heavy emphasis on bowling strength in the side chosen on Sunday.

— *CANBERRA TIMES*, 10 JULY 1968

LAWRY ALONE IN HIS JOY

'We came here to hold the Ashes and we have succeeded', a smiling Australian tour captain, Bill Lawry, exclaimed in the Headingley pavilion last night. There were few to share his enthusiasm in the after match scenes of an anticlimactic finish of the drawn fourth Test match.

— *CANBERRA TIMES*, 1 AUGUST 1968

GRIM STAND BY LAWRY IN TEST

Bill Lawry, in the most gallant innings of his career, batted throughout a tense third day of the fifth cricket Test against England at The Oval yesterday for an unbeaten 135. Lawry fought tenaciously for six hours to keep Australia's hopes alive of averting the follow-on. At the end of a day of high tension, Australia had reached a total of 7/264 in reply to England's mammoth first innings 494.

Tomorrow, the fourth day, Australia, with three wickets standing and Lawry a refreshed giant, needs 31 runs to save the follow-on. The Oval pitch is showing its first signs of fractiousness and the odds are all in favour of England in the Test, which they must win to level the series. Ian Redpath stayed to make 67 and share a sturdy stand of 125 runs with his captain. But when Redpath departed, Australia's total at a healthy 136, the rot set in. Ian Chappell (10), Doug Walters (5), Paul Sheahan (14), and Barry Jarman (0) surrendered with irresponsible, panicky stroke-play.

— *CANBERRA TIMES*, 26 AUGUST 1968

IAN REDPATH

In late 1969, the team's accommodation became an issue again during our five Test tour of India. There were good hotels available in India but, unfortunately, the Board chose not to billet us in any of them. We grumbled a fair bit about the accommodation that the Board put us in, but, on the field, we got on with it and had a wonderful tour.

The cricket was some of the best that we ever played. The pitches turned and India deployed at least three quality spinners in every Test. It was an even contest between bat and ball. Both sides bowled well and the batsmen had to treat good bowling with respect. Anything over 200 in a day was a good day for the batting team. Three hundred in an innings was practically a match-winning total. It was an absorbing series to play in and we had to be at our best to win 3–1.

We experienced our first crowd riot of the tour on the fourth evening of the first Test at Brabourne Stadium in Bombay after a radio commentator questioned the umpire's decision to give Srinivas Venkataraghavan out caught behind. (Ironically, Venkat himself later went on to become an accomplished Test umpire.) A section of the crowd started chucking Coke bottles onto the ground. Smoke soon enveloped the ground. We all informed Bill that we didn't want to field on the boundary. We all wanted to field in the circle. It's the only time in my career that I heard blokes volunteering to field at short leg.

The army came out at mid-wicket and turned to face the rioting crowd. The soldiers picked up the Coke bottles and threw them as hard as they could back into the crowd. Meanwhile, we were still playing! Then the scorer ran out onto the field with his book under his arm. 'I'm the scorer,' he said to Bill. 'I can't see.' So he went over and started to score in the Members' Stand.

The riot kept getting worse. Pretty soon, we had to get off the field. Keith Stackpole and Ashley Mallett did so armed with stumps for self-defence. By this point, the unrest had even spread to the Members' Stand. So the soldiers lined up in front of the stand as we were coming off the ground and charged into it while we ran down the tunnel into our dressing room.

That wasn't the end of it. When we got back to our dressing room, Bill got hit by two wicker chairs dropped from the balcony above and John Gleeson got hit in the head by a bottle. The rioters chucked bottles at our dressing room windows, smashing every single one, and we retreated upstairs to the safety of the rooms at the Cricket Club of India where we were staying. 'Crikey,' I thought to myself, 'it's only the first Test. We've got another eight games to go in India. This is going to be interesting.'

The second Test was in Kanpur. We stayed at the Kamala Retreat. For security, we had soldiers stationed on each corner of the building with bayonets fixed to their rifles. When we travelled to and from Green Park stadium for the Test, we were flanked by two army trucks, one in front and one behind our team bus.

There was no riot at Green Park, but you had to have your wits about you when you were out on the field. Spectators would insert a skyrocket into a Coke bottle,

lay the bottle on the ground with its base pointing towards the intended target and set off the skyrocket. The bottle-rocket would scuttle across the ground like a snake at about 50 miles an hour. These bottle-rockets were generally fired in the direction of the cricketers on the field. You had to make sure to lift your leg as the bottle-rocket scuttled past, lest you acquire a painful foot injury.

It was a bit different from the MCG, but a great adventure.

I learned long ago that any game you play, you must play to win. To be successful and win cricket matches you must have a team of 11 players who are prepared to play for their team and not for themselves.
— Bill Lawry

MEMBERS OF THE AUSTRALIAN CRICKET TEAM IN LONDON (LEFT TO RIGHT) IAN REDPATH, GRAHAM MCKENZIE, BOB COWPER, ALAN CONNOLLY, PAUL SHEAHAN, NEIL HAWKE, IAN CHAPPELL, ERIC FREEMAN, JOHN INVERARITY, DAVE RENNEBERG, ASHLEY MALLETT, JOHN GLEESON, LES JOSLIN, DOUG WALTERS, BRIAN TABER AND BILL LAWRY. (PA IMAGES VIA GETTY IMAGES)

AUSTRALIAN CAPTAIN, BILL LAWRY, IN 1968.
(AUSTRALIAN NEWS AND INFORMATION BUREAU/NATIONAL ARCHIVES)

KEITH STACKPOLE

In late January 1966, I made my Test debut as a 25-year-old against England at Adelaide Oval. England's captain, Mike Smith, won the toss and batted. We bowled England out for 241 early on the second day, thanks largely to Graham McKenzie who took 6/48 after initially being dropped for the Test, only to be reprieved when his replacement, Peter Allan, succumbed to injury.

I spent the rest of the day with my feet up in the dressing room watching Bill and Simmo go about their work. It was my first time watching them open in a Test match. Together, they batted like a perfectly tuned, precision-engineered machine. It was beautiful to watch. It was a typically hot and dry Australia Day weekend in Adelaide and they first nullified then completely demoralised the English attack.

They put on a masterclass in how to run between the wickets. They pinched every single available, thereby constantly rotating the strike and keeping the scoreboard ticking over. They treated the good balls with respect and punished the bad balls. Each of them scored at a strike-rate in excess of 50 without taking any undue risks. I can't recall either of them giving the English a genuine chance until Bill was bowled by Fred Titmus for 119 off 217 balls in the final session, by which time our team's total was 244. We went on to win the Test by an innings and 9 runs with a day to spare.

At that stage, Simmo was Australian captain. Two years later, Bill took over from Simmo. Three years after that, Ian Chappell took over from Bill. So I had the privilege of playing under three Australian Test captains. They were all good captains with different strengths and weaknesses. Philosophically, Bill and Simmo belonged to the same school of thought. When they walked out on the field, their first priority was: we don't want to lose. You have to understand that, back in those days, Australia losing a Test match was one of the worst things that could happen. Ian practised an entirely different philosophy. His first priority was always to win the Test match and he was happy to risk losing in order to do so.

Bill was a very good and astute captain. He led by example. As such, he was a terrific leader of mature cricketers who knew their own game and young fellas finding their way in Shield or Test cricket. The personality type that posed a bit more of a challenge for Bill was fellas like Doug Walters who needed the reins to be left off them. Because Bill was so dedicated to cricket, he didn't quite know how to handle blokes like Dougie who, instead of going to bed early the night before a game, needed a beer or two to relax and perform at their best the next day.

AUSTRALIA PLAYS THE WEST INDIES IN
1969 AND BILL LAWRY CLIPS A BALL FROM
GARRY SOBERS. (AUSTRALIAN NEWS AND
INFORMATION BUREAU/NATIONAL ARCHIVES)

Ian, on the other hand, was great at handling blokes like Dougie, but probably not as good as Bill at handling young blokes who needed the reins drawn in a fraction. The example that always springs to my mind is David Hookes. I reckon that if Hookesy had had a year or two under Bill's captaincy when he first got into the Australian team, his Test career would've panned out a bit differently.

When Simmo retired from Test cricket in early January 1968, Bill had a readymade replacement as his Test opening partner in Ian Redpath. Bill and Redders had been opening together successfully for Victoria for years and had already opened together on seven occasions at Test level.

A year later, we played the third Test of a five Test series against the West Indies at the SCG. I was still making my way in Test cricket. It was my 10th Test and I'd only passed 50 once. I'd batted everywhere from four to eight. I just hadn't managed to nail down a position in Australia's batting order.

About 25 minutes before lunch on the second day, we bowled the West Indies out for 264. 'Ah,' I thought to myself as we started walking off the SCG, 'I'll put my feet up for the rest of the day and I might get a hit sometime tomorrow.' I was about 30 yards from the gates to the pavilion when Bill walked up to me and said, 'Put the pads on'.

'What do you want – a lunch watchman?' I replied.

'No, you're opening.'

I was shocked. Redders was in the team and I naturally assumed that he'd be opening with Bill. When the three of us played together for Victoria, Bill and Redders opened and I batted three. I didn't even open for Collingwood, usually batting three or four.

Bill's unconventional decision soon looked like a masterstroke. He and I put on a solid opening partnership of 68. I got 58 off 80 balls. Redders, batting at four, scored 80 off 132 balls. And Australia won the Test by 10 wickets. For the next two years, I opened with Bill in nearly every Test that we played together and Redders batted in the middle order.

Bill's decision to promote me to open that afternoon in Sydney was the best thing that ever happened to my

TEST RECORDS GO AS AUSTRALIANS TAKE CHARGE

Graham McKenzie, Bill Lawry and Ian Chappell rewrote the record book to the enchantment of 28,000 rapt enthusiasts at the MCG today, and gave Australia a wonderful chance of taking the second Test.

Australia's commanding position at stumps is almost entirely due to these three — Lawry for his brave and triumphant decision to let the visitors bat first and his century; Chappell for his fifth century in five matches against the West Indies; and McKenzie for doing what no other fast bowler has achieved in the 300-plus Test matches Australia has played: taking eight wickets in a single innings. Indeed it was all Australia today, from the first over, and the last Friday of 1968 will be one day the cavaliers from the Caribbean will gladly forget.

Lawry and Chappell for the second time in two matches came together in a great double-century partnership. They smashed the second wicket partnership record for Australia against the West Indies, which many of those at the MCG today would have seen Bradman and Ponsford compile on a similar sunny afternoon against the first West Indian tourists, here just 37 years ago.

— ROHAN RIVETT, *CANBERRA TIMES*, 28 DEC 1968

cricket career. It only took a few overs for me to realise that, for an aggressive hitter like me, opening was a lot easier than batting in the middle order. As an opener, if I played a good shot, I got a boundary. When I hit that same shot batting in the middle-order, there was usually a fielder there to keep it to one or a dot.

I was a tad lucky when I opened for the first time alongside Bill that afternoon at the SCG. You will not find a more attacking captain than the West Indies' Garry Sobers. He had third man and fine leg up to maximise his number of catchers behind the wicket. When his bowlers dropped a bit short, I was able to cut or hook them for boundaries. I quickly motored to my half-century and never looked back. Opening became my cricket life. I started opening for Victoria and Collingwood too.

Bill is one of my closest mates, but I must confess that I've never asked him how or why he made the decision to promote me to open. I don't even know if the decision was his alone or one that he made in consultation with the selectors. (Back in those days, the selectors usually picked a team in batting order.) Although, at first glance, the decision seemed strange given that Redders was a specialist opener and I was not, there was actually a lot of logic to the decision. Redders wasn't getting many runs opening for Australia. I wasn't getting many runs down the order. And it was obvious that I was a back-foot player who enjoyed playing quick bowling.

Bill's decision to install me as his Test opening partner was great for my career, but I firmly believe that it was detrimental to his. Before me, Bill's two Test opening partners had been Simmo and Redders. Like Bill, Simmo and Redders were technically proficient openers who were adept at working the ball into gaps and looking for quick singles. Thus, when Bill opened with them, the strike was constantly rotated and the scoreboard ticked over with the regularity of a grandfather clock.

But, when I started out as a Test opener, I was very different from Simmo and Redders. I was a boundary hitter. I was not good at looking for singles. Sometimes, we'd be 0/40 and I'd be on 33 and Bill would be on five or six. Even Bill, with his legendary patience, started to get agitated in that situation. (When he opened with

Simmo and Redders, he never got agitated – because constant singles rotated the strike.) So, he started taking the odd risk or two and got out.

When Bill opened with me in his last 17 Tests, he only averaged 39.42. Before that, he'd averaged 49.75 in his first 50 Tests. That drop in performance was largely due to my inability to find singles.

Of course, there were times when Bill's famously aggressive running between the wickets resulted in a run-out. On one occasion in early December 1968, he was involved in three run-outs in the space of about 20 minutes. Victoria was playing Western Australia at the MCG. We'd seized a 63 run first innings lead and were batting to set WA a target. Bill and Redders opened, as they usually did for Victoria and Australia at that time, and put on 175 before Redders was bowled by Sam Gannon for 92.

I joined Bill out in the middle. He was in the 80s and looked certain to get a century. A few minutes later, Bill was on strike at the Southern End. He hit a firm drive along the ground straight to cover and called 'Yes!'

'No, go back!' I immediately replied.

It was too late. He was already about a third of the way down the pitch. He stopped, turned around and took a few steps back towards his crease before giving up when he saw that the keeper had already taken the bails off. He started walking slowly back to the pavilion at the Members' end. Meanwhile, I'm standing about a yard out of my crease at the Members' end, upset at the fact I'd been involved in running out my mate when he was within sight of a hundred. A few seconds later, Bill walked past me.

At that point, the umpire, Bill Smyth, called him back and said, 'Bill, you're not out. Stack, you're out.'

'What?' I said. 'You're joking!'

He wasn't. Since Bill and I had crossed, I was run out for three.

That brought Paul Sheahan to the crease. About five minutes later, Bill ran Paul out for two. I was sitting in the pavilion next to our number six, Les Joslin. 'He won't run me out', said Les. About 10 minutes later, Les walked out to join Bill in the middle after our number five, John Grant, was bowled by Graham McKenzie for seven. Les returned to the pavilion a few minutes later, having been run out by Bill for a duck!

Next in was Peter 'Wheels' Bedford, a future Brownlow medallist who was the fastest runner in our team. Wheels backed up about halfway down the pitch whenever Bill was on strike. About five minutes later, Bill reached his century and promptly declared at 5/221, setting the Sandgropers 285 to win.

Usually, when a batsman scores a century, he gets a round of applause from his teammates when he arrives back in the dressing room. Ray 'Slug' Jordon, our keeper, suggested that we play a prank on Bill. 'Let's all hide in the showers', he said. When Bill arrived back in our dressing room, it was empty. After about five minutes, we all returned and casually congratulated him on his hundred. 'Well played Phan', said the boys with their tongues firmly in their cheeks.

Bill didn't bat an eyelid. He was completely unperturbed and just got on with it. He even managed a little pep talk before we went back out on the field. 'C'mon,' he said, 'we've got to get out there and knock these blokes over to get the outright win', with no mention of the run-outs or an apology.

The tale of the three run-outs is a funny story that we all still like to joke about, but it actually tells you something important about Bill. Mentally, he was the strongest batsman I ever saw. His ability to concentrate and bat for long periods of time was simply incredible. On so many occasions, I saw him bat through an entire day for Victoria or Australia without his concentration ever wavering. He could block out the noise and just bat … and bat and bat. That's why he scored so many runs for Northcote, Victoria and Australia.

GARRY SOBERS POURS CHAMPAGNE FOR BILL LAWRY IN 1969. (AUSTRALIAN NEWS AND INFORMATION BUREAU/NATIONAL ARCHIVES)

TEST CAPTAIN ACCUSED
'NO KNOWLEDGE' OF BLOW BY LAWRY

The Australian cricket team manager, Mr Bennett, said today he knew nothing of accusations that captain Bill Lawry had hit an Indian press photographer during yesterday's fourth Test.

A meeting of the Indian Press Photographers Association last night said Lawry had hit one photographer and abused another while they were taking photographs on the Eden Gardens ground when about 5,000 fans rushed the wicket. 'Bill has said nothing to me and I have not heard anything from the photographers', Mr Bennett said. 'I certainly didn't see anything happen, but it was impossible to see anything very clearly. There were about 5,000 people all over the ground and there were photographers running around everywhere. The only thing I can think of is that Bill may have pushed some people back from the wicket and maybe a photographer was one of them. I know I went out to the ground and pushed plenty of people myself to try to get the ground cleared so the game could go on.' Mr Bennett said he had no intention of investigating the claims until he heard directly from the photographers.

'As far as I am concerned this is just an unconfirmed report', he said. 'None of the boys have mentioned anything like this.' Lawry has made no public comment on the report.

— *Canberra Times*, 18 December 1969

LAWRY'S TEAM SET A DUBIOUS TEST REPUTATION

Skipper Bill Lawry's men lost four Test matches in a row against South Africa and won only four of eight regional matches, drawing the remainder. The opportunity the Springboks gained to hone their young players to a fine edge after a three year absence from Test cricket gives them a good chance of victory in their British tour, aside from the unpredictable factor of threatening anti-apartheid demonstrations. For the Australians, the tour meant that many players may have to demonstrate their ability afresh for the 1970–71 season. Such players as Graham McKenzie, Keith Stackpole and Brian Taber fared poorly in the Tests, and sports writers here believed skipper Bill Lawry's tarnished prestige could weigh against him for future selection.

— *Canberra Times*, 24 March 1970

KEITH STACKPOLE

Bill was never a big talker when we were batting together. The one notable exception was the 1969 tour of India. Our team played really well, winning the five Test series 3–1. But there was a fair bit of drama off-the-field, with multiple crowd riots during the Tests. The second riot, which occurred on the afternoon of the fourth day of the fourth Test at Eden Gardens in Kolkata, was particularly memorable.

We needed 39 runs to win the Test and take a 2–1 series lead. After about five overs, we were just one run from victory. In one section of the stands, the spectators on the top deck started throwing chairs, bottles and things on the people in the lower deck who, understandably, rushed onto the ground to escape the onslaught.

In response to this ground invasion, the Indian team walked off. Bill and I stayed right where we were out in the middle. 'We're not going to leave', Bill calmly told me. His reasoning was simple: if we went off, he was worried that we'd never get back on to complete our victory. That brief chat was, by far, the longest that Bill ever had with me out in the middle.

Somehow, a photographer with a box Brownie camera made his way out into the middle and started trying to snap photos of us. I have no idea how he got there. He kept trying to get in front of us to take a close-up photo. We kept turning our backs to him in order to make it hard for him to take his photo and thereby encourage him to leave the ground. Eventually, he managed to get in front of us and snap his photo. 'Now, get off the ground!' said Bill. 'Go on, get off!' He then gently nudged the photographer in the back with his bat and said 'Get off!'

The photographer stumbled and fell forwards onto his camera which dug into his ribs. Suddenly, the next day in the paper, you see a photo of Bill with his bat up in the air with this photographer on the ground writhing in pain and it looks as though he's king hit him! In fact, Bill barely touched the bloke.

Play stopped as Bill and I stood out in the middle without the Indian team. After 13 minutes, the Indian team returned to the field. Fortunately, their captain, the Nawab of Pataudi, was a sensible bloke. He went up to Bill and said, 'We've got to get off the ground. I've told Guha to bowl a full toss.' Subrata Guha was India's right-arm quick.

Bill approached me and said, 'Guha's going to bowl you a full toss. Just nudge it into the covers for a single and we'll get off.' As Guha was running in, I thought, 'Wow, for the first time in my life, I know I'm going to get a full toss.' When it arrived, I smashed it for four.

'Why'd you do that?' asked Bill.

'You would've done exactly the same thing if you knew

I said to my wife – when I met her, I was 19 years old and I was playing for Victoria – this will last only five or six years, this cricket.
— Bill Lawry

The happiest moment of the day for me is when I drive into the driveway of my house. That applied when I was single, when I was married and it remains to this day.
— Bill Lawry

you were getting a full toss', I replied. 'You wouldn't have just nudged it for one. You would've plonked it for four!'

We all started walking off the ground. As we approached the pavilion, some spectators in the Members' Stand started throwing things at Pataudi. It was clear that a pretty ugly situation was brewing. It wasn't Pataudi's fault. It was December 1969, the height of the Cold War, and the Vietnam War raged on. Kolkata was a communist stronghold. Everywhere we went in the city, we saw the hammer and sickle flag. Pataudi, an aristocrat by birth, was never going to be popular with the crowd in a communist city, especially when he'd just lost a Test match. We suggested to Pataudi that he walk between us and, as we walked up the races, we put our bats together over his head to shield him from the crowd.

The next day, on our way to the airport, our bus was stoned by an angry mob. Someone left a window open and a rock about the size of my hand flew in and missed Johnny Gleeson by a matter of inches before shattering a window on the opposite side of the bus.

Still, we'd won the Test, so we were happy! What we weren't happy about was the quality of the accommodation that the Australian Cricket Board put us in. There were good hotels in India. We just didn't stay in them. The accommodation that the Board put us in was shocking. You wouldn't let a pig loose in some of those places.

Nevertheless, we kept playing well on the field, winning the fifth and final Test in Madras (now Chennai) by 77 runs to clinch the series 3–1.

Then, instead of going home, we flew straight to South Africa for a four Test series against a South African side featuring Barry Richards, Graeme Pollock and Mike Procter that many rated the best in the world. We were exhausted and were deservedly beaten 4–0. Dissatisfaction at the Board's pathetic handling of our travel arrangements and accommodation, which had been steadily growing since the start of the tour of India, peaked during the tour of South Africa when the Board tried to schedule an extra Test match, which would've brought the total number of Tests we played on the back-to-back tours of India and South Africa to 10. We asked

for an extra $500. The Board countered with an offer of $200 which we rejected. We'd had enough and refused to play the extra Test.

We had a team meeting where we all got our complaints off our chests. Bill patiently listened to every single complaint then said, 'Ok, I'm going to send a letter to the Board setting out all our major complaints and the problems that we experienced'.

'I think we should all sign the letter', suggested Redders. The team would've been happy to do so, but Bill in his wisdom – or, if you're a cynic, lack thereof – said, 'No, I'm captain. I'll sign it.' That was Bill. As a leader, he took responsibility.

So Bill signed the letter himself and sent it off to the Board. I've always believed that, politically, that act of leadership caused his downfall as Australian captain. Once the Board received the letter, they started looking for a reason to sack him and the following Australian summer, they got it.

I was walking through the gate with Bob [Cowper] and he was a bit down and I said, 'What's wrong?' and he said, 'We're getting paid 2 pound 10 a day. We play for nothing'. He said, 'See Jack on the sight screen? He's in the Miscellaneous Workers' Union and he's on time-and-a-half, getting 8 pound 50!' Bob Cowper was far more intelligent than I. I still went out and blocked all day for 2 pound 10.
— Bill Lawry

GRAHAM McKENZIE

After India, we jetted to South Africa for a four Test series against a South African team that many rated the best in the world. Neither Bill nor I knew it at the time, but it would be the final Test tour for both of us. By that late stage in his career, Bill had acquired a reputation as a somewhat staid batsman and captain. But off-the-field, Bill had actually gotten funnier and more confident in his powers of joke- and story-telling over the years.

I had some mates in South Africa – because that 1970 tour of South Africa was my second and I'd met quite a few South Africans during a season of county cricket with Leicestershire – so, during that tour, I'd sometimes get asked if I'd like to come out to dinner. Typically, the verbal invitation would include the line 'oh, and bring one of your teammates with you.' To which I'd reply, 'Sure, I'll see who's available.' When I came back and told them that Bill was available you could see the crestfallen look on their faces. (Presumably, they were hoping for Dougie Walters!) But when they'd drop us off at our hotel at the end of a very entertaining and enjoyable evening, they'd always say, 'Gee, Bill Lawry is a lot different from what I thought!'

ARTICLES BY LAWRY 'NOT APPROVED'

The Australian Cricket Board of Control has informed Indian cricket authorities that articles by the Australian captain, Bill Lawry, about the last tour of India were written without the board's prior knowledge or approval. 'We do not condone such action, but unfortunately the modern press not only accepts but appears to demand "journalistic licence" in its presentation of events'. During the past winter's series, won 3–1 by Australia, Indian papers criticised Lawry and other players for alleged rudeness to umpires and unsporting behaviour. Lawry's press articles hit back at these criticisms. The Australian letter, while expressing regret that the articles had caused concern, said Lawry was at perfect liberty to write for the Press.

— *Canberra Times*, 17 September 1970

LAWRY OUT 'TO FIND FORM'

'It's open slather this cricket season and all players realise they will have to be on their mettle from the word go', Victorian captain Bill Lawry said on the eve of the first Sheffield match this season against Western Australia at the Melbourne Cricket Ground tomorrow. 'The pressure will be on every Australian cricketer in the matches leading up to the first Test in Brisbane on November 27', he said.

— *Canberra Times*, 30 October 1970

LAWRY UNDER FIRE FOR CAPTAINCY IN TEST

For the first time since the Johnson–Miller controversy of the mid-50s there must be some thought to the possible necessity of a change in the Australian captaincy during a series.

Bill Lawry's captaincy and especially his handling of the Australian attack this weekend at the SCG will come under widespread censure. Unhappily for Lawry, one of the greatest opening batsmen in Australian Test history, these doubts arise at a time when his own stroke-making seems to have fallen away almost catastrophically.

— Rohan Rivett, *Canberra Times*, 11 January 1971

CROWD JEERS AS LAWRY DECLARES, SETS AUSTRALIA FOR VICTORY

After a great day for Australia, in which the partisan Melbourne crowd found a new idol and luck again ran consistently Australia's way, the skipper was booed after 5pm when he declared the Australian innings closed with Australia's new 'keeper Rodney Marsh just eight runs short of a first Test century.

Lawry was right — without qualification or apology. After the Sydney drubbing last week, any Australian captain had only one obligation to Australia, to cricket and his own team — to square the series.

— Rohan Rivett, *Canberra Times*, 23 January 1971

KEITH STACKPOLE

We took on a strong England side in a seven Test home Ashes series. The first two Tests were drawn, the third Test was abandoned without a ball being bowled because of torrential rain, the fourth Test was lost by 299 runs and the fifth Test was drawn. So, the sixth Test, played at Adelaide Oval from late January to early February 1971, was crucial. We had to win the Test to keep alive the possibility of winning the series.

In the end, we claimed a fighting draw after conceding a 235 run first innings deficit. I thought that it was a decent result. If we won the final Test, we'd draw the series and retain the Ashes.

The morning after the Test, Redders and I were in our Adelaide motel room when the phone rang. I answered. It was Alan Shiell, a South Australian Shield cricketer turned cricket journalist for *The Advertiser*.

'Is Bill Lawry there?' he asked.

'I don't think so', I replied. 'I think he's out visiting some pigeon fanciers. What's news?'

'There's been a few changes in the Test team', answered Alan. 'Bill Lawry's been dropped.'

'What!' I exclaimed.

'Ian Chappell's captain and Bill's been dropped', said Alan.

I was shocked. I finished up the call with Alan and hung up the phone. Redders heard everything. 'God,' he said, 'Phanto's been dropped. How are we going to tell him?'

At that moment, there was a knock on our door and in walked Bill. 'Phant,' I said, 'you better sit down.'

'Why?' he replied quick as a flash. 'Have I been dropped?'

'Yes, you have', we both said.

'Mmmm, I thought I may have been in trouble', he said calmly. 'The selectors didn't say a word to me after the Test.' Usually, the selectors spoke to the captain after a Test to ask him how the Test went and get his thoughts about the best XI for the next Test.

Bill copped his dropping on the chin. He never lost his composure. When we got off the plane at Melbourne Airport, there were heaps of press people around and Bill calmly answered all their questions.

That, unfortunately, was the end of Bill's Test career. We'd never play another Test together.

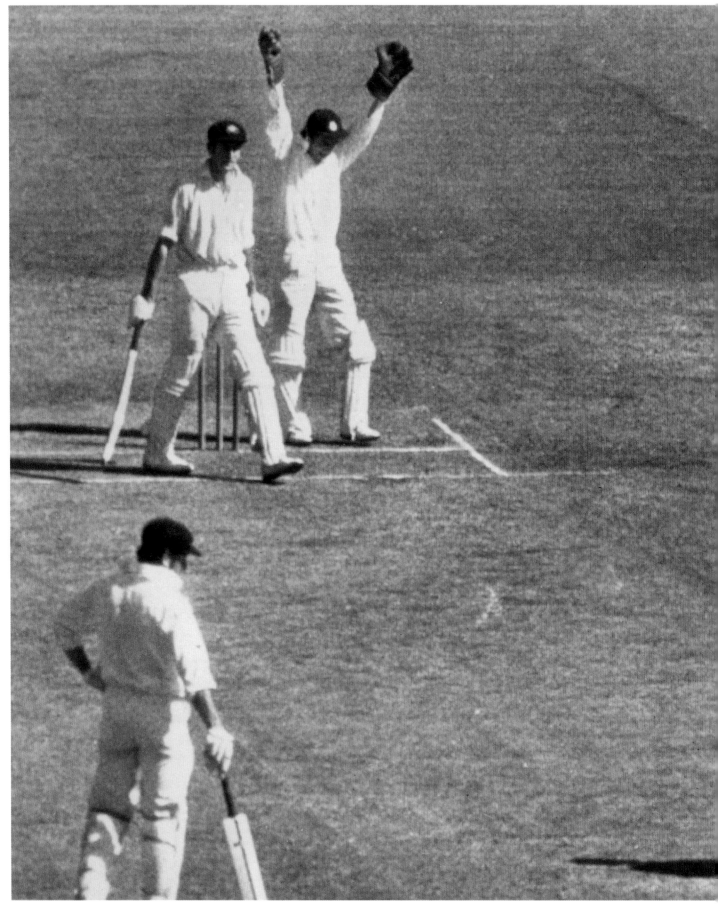

Bill was a wonderful, courageous batsman and a good, safe fieldsman. As captain he was terrific, so long as he had genuine fast bowlers and a medium-paced workhorse of the Alan Connolly type at his disposal, he was in his element. Some spinners – like yours truly – were not Bill's cup of tea. He wanted things as tight as a drum; a four hit from a spinner seemed tantamount to treason.
— Ashley Mallett

AUSTRALIA CAPTAIN BILL LAWRY IS OUT FOR 27 AFTER BEING CAUGHT BY ALAN KNOTT OFF RAY ILLINGWORTH DURING THE FIRST ONE DAY INTERNATIONAL (ODI) BETWEEN AUSTRALIA AND ENGLAND AT THE MELBOURNE CRICKET GROUND IN 1971. AUSTRALIA WON THE GAME BY 5 WICKETS. (PHOTO BY KEYSTONE/HULTON ARCHIVE/GETTY IMAGES)

IAN REDPATH

At the conclusion of our two month, five Test tour of India, we flew straight to South Africa for a four Test series against a South African team featuring Graeme Pollock, Barry Richards and Mike Procter. They walloped us 4–0. They were too good for us. They were a mighty team, probably the best side in the world by a stretch at the time, and played extremely well in that series.

Procter was a spectacular fast bowler. He ran in flat out from about a thirty yards. He was quick and he was aggressive. Peter Pollock was probably one of the most underrated Test fast bowlers ever. And then you had to deal with their magnificent batting line-up.

Normally, we were a good fielding unit, but in that series, we dropped a lot of catches. That, to me, was a sign that we were a bit fatigued mentally after an intense five Test tour of India. That's not an excuse for our performance in South Africa. The Springboks – as they were known then – outplayed us and deserved to win. Against a team that good, we had to be 100 per cent mentally switched on to have any chance of victory. Instead, we were probably only 80 per cent mentally switched on, partly because of the rigours of the tour of India and partly because the South Africans were such a brilliant team that they didn't allow us to find the remaining 20 per cent of our powers of concentration.

Our dissatisfaction with the Board's handling of our travel and accommodation arrangements had been building since the tour of India. It all came to a boil during the tour of South Africa when the Board asked us to play an extra Test. We discussed the Board's request as a team and put what we thought was a fair price on what would've been a 10th Test on the back-to-back tours of India and South Africa: $500. The Board countered with an offer of $200, which we rejected. No extra Test was played.

Towards the end of the tour, we had a team meeting where we all spoke about our complaints regarding the Board's handling of our travel and accommodation arrangements. As captain, Bill dutifully listened to our complaints and penned a letter to the Board summarising them. He showed us the letter. I, along with some of the other lads, suggested that we all sign it. Everyone was happy to sign it. But Bill said, 'I'm the captain. I'll sign it.'

It was a letter that had to be written. Unfortunately, my understanding is that it wasn't very well received by the Board. Politically, Bill's card had been marked. Midway through the following home summer, the summer of 1970–71, a team rebuild was decided upon, changes were made and he was dropped from the side.

That summer, we faced a very good England side in a seven Test home Ashes series. We were 1–0 down heading into the must-win sixth Test played at Adelaide Oval from late January to early February 1971. We drew the Test and thereby eliminated the prospect of winning the series.

The morning after the Test, Stack and I were in our Adelaide motel room waiting to go to the airport. Stack got a call from Alan Shiell, a South Australian Shield cricketer turned cricket journalist for *The Advertiser*, who informed him that Bill had been sacked. I was shocked. Bill had been one of our better batsmen that series, averaging 40.50. He was still the one who stood up when things were tough. If one of us had stayed with him in the final innings of the fourth Test at the SCG, when he carried his bat against John Snow on a deteriorating final day pitch for an unbeaten 60, we'd have drawn the Test and there wouldn't have been any basis for sacking him.

Moments later, Bill came into our room and we broke the news of his sacking to him. He took it remarkably well, remaining calm and composed. We travelled together on the same flight back to Melbourne where the nation's media awaited him. Never once did he lose his composure. He calmly answered all the questions that the press had for him. He didn't cut loose on anybody. There were no sour grapes.

It was Bill's final performance as Australian captain and it turned out to be one of his very best.

ENGLAND CAPTAIN, RAY ILLINGWORTH, TALKS TO THE UMPIRE AFTER BOWLER JOHN SNOW (LEFT) WAS WARNED OVER BOWLING TOO MANY SHORT-PITCHED DELIVERIES DURING THE 1971 TEST AT PERTH. SNOW AND BILL LAWRY AWAIT THE OUTCOME. (CENTRAL PRESS/HULTON ARCHIVE/GETTY IMAGES)

ROLAND PERRY

From *Captain Australia*

In South Africa in 1969–70, the wheels fell off the Australian winning train. It was thrashed in each of the four Tests. Bill Lawry had his worst series yet, scoring just 193 at 24.13. It was a form aberration, but it put his captaincy in jeopardy.

He lost it during the next Ashes series in Australia in 1970–71, when Australia went down nil–two in six Tests against the equally obdurate Ray Illingworth and his strong squad. The English team included hostile, effective speedster John Snow with the ball, and Geoff Boycott, England's answer to Lawry. Bill Lawry's form was steady, but his stodginess at the crease had turned off observers, including selectors. This was despite his gritty bat carrying for 60 not out of his team's pitiful 116 at Sydney. His steady aggregate of 324 at 40.5 was not enough to save him.

Lawry was sacked following a draw in Adelaide and Ian Chappell took over as skipper in the final game at the Sydney Cricket Ground. No one from the Board of Control bothered to inform Lawry and he received the news from teammate Keith Stackpole, who heard an item on the radio en route to the airport. Lawry, just turned thirty-four, had been dumped from the last Test.

Lawry was also a shock omission from the tour of England in 1972. Critics felt he should have been on tour, especially as no one could fill his place. While Keith Stackpole had a good series, he had no partner who could stay with him. Opening stands were woeful. Just one was more than 24 runs. Perhaps there was a case for leaving Ian Chappell unfettered by not having his former leader looking over his shoulder. Yet both men seemed secure enough not to cause a problem. The 1972 Ashes was tight, with each side winning twice. Lawry's inclusion would have swung it Australia's way.

But it wasn't to be. Bill Lawry went out of Test cricket with an aggregate of 5234 runs at 47.15, with thirteen centuries – seven against England and four versus the West Indies. In first-class cricket he scored 18,734 at 50.9, with fifty centuries and 100 fifties, which showed his importance at the top of the order.

LAWRY OUT: 'THE BOLDEST DECISION IN CRICKET'

Australia's selectors today made one of the boldest decisions in the history of Australian Test cricket by dropping captain Bill Lawry for the seventh and decisive Test in Sydney next Friday.

Never before in this century has an Australian captain been dropped during the course of a series in Australia.

Great sympathy must go out from every thinking cricket-lover – we may omit the beer can rattlers and the inebriated 'avagoyamug' loudmouths – to Bill Lawry. For a decade, since he first opened in England in June 1961 and played that immortal innings at Lord's, he has been an automatic selection in the Australian XI and most 'world' elevens. His Test career was not three weeks old when he was on the front page of every paper in the Commonwealth after his heroic century on 'the ridge' pitch at Lord's against the thunderbolts of Trueman and company. In the West Indies against Hall and Griffith, and again in Australia against Brown, Jones and Higgs, Bill Lawry and Bob Simpson wrote new figures in the Test record book for Australian opening partnerships. Several times through the 60s Lawry stood second only to Bradman in Australian Test averages. As captain his record was splendid until the beginning of last year when the South Africans wrung our withers with four devastating defeats in a row. It was at this time that stories of dissension in the Australian team and of criticism of Lawry's captaincy and handling of his bowlers began.

— ROHAN RIVETT, *CANBERRA TIMES*, 5 FEBRUARY 1971

BILL LAWRY AND THE ENGLAND CAPTAIN RAY ILLINGWORTH TOSS A COIN ON THE MELBOURNE CRICKET GROUND. (PHOTO BY HULTON/GETTY IMAGES)

NEIL HARVEY

On his maiden Ashes tour, Bill's attacking batsmanship had been instrumental to our series win. I'll never forget his performances at Lord's and Old Trafford – they were absolutely brilliant. But, as the years went on, he became more and more defensive as a batsman. And when he was appointed Australia's 32nd Test captain in January 1968, he became a defensive captain too.

Now, to be fair, he wasn't blessed with the world's greatest bowling resources. He only had one world-class fast bowler – Graham McKenzie – and he didn't have a single world-class spinner. So he set out to not lose Tests, rather than win them.

I must admit that, as an Australian selector during that period, he did drive us up the wall a bit with that approach! When, in late January 1971, we dropped him from the Australian captaincy and the Australian team, one of our main reasons was that he'd simply become too defensive as a batsman and a captain. Australian cricket at that time needed a shot in the arm. Crowds were down. And we knew that Bill's replacement as captain,

Ian Chappell, would play the kind of attacking cricket that we and the Australian public wanted.

It was a difficult decision to make because Bill is a mate who I'd watched grow from a kid riding his bicycle around the humble, industrial suburb of Thornbury into a world-class Test batsman and Australia's 32nd Test captain. Bill, to his credit, never held a grudge against me for that decision.

Besides, nothing can ever change the fact that Bill was one of Australia's best and bravest opening batsmen. He was a great fighter. I enjoyed every minute that I played with and toured alongside him. He was a wonderful teammate and remains a good friend.

AUSTRALIAN CAPTAIN, BILL LAWRY.
(NEWSPIX)

BILL LAWRY
(TRINITY MIRROR/MIRRORPIX/ALAMY)

MARTIN WILLIAMSON

The end of a Victorian hero

In 1971 Bill Lawry became the first Australian captain to be sacked in the middle of a series ... and he paid the price for negativity and daring to challenge the authority of the Australian board

The 1970–71 Ashes series has gone down in history as not only cricket's longest – there were seven Tests including the washed out Melbourne game – but also as one of the most acrimonious. It was also the first time that ABC had broadcast ball-by-ball television coverage throughout Australia. The final Test at Sydney marked the low, with Ray Illingworth leading the England side from the field after the crowd threw bottles and cans at John Snow.

In that match Australia were playing for the first time under the captaincy of Ian Chappell. Their captain for the previous six Tests, and for three years before that, had been Bill Lawry. But after a draw in the sixth Test at Adelaide, Lawry had been unceremoniously dumped by the selectors, the first Australian skipper to be sacked during a series. So badly was he treated that he found out from fellow opener Keith Stackpole, who had himself been told by a former teammate.

This was no ordinary dismissal, however. Australia were only one down, and as Australia held the Ashes, all they needed was to win the last game against a tired England side to retain them. What is more, Lawry, a virtual fixture in the side since 1961, had not had a bad series with the bat, scoring 324 runs in five Tests at 40.50. On the face of it, it seemed a callous decision.

But behind the scenes, Lawry had hardly courted popularity either on or off the pitch. As a captain he had started well, retaining the Ashes in England in a disappointing series, but that was followed with a tremendous series win against West Indies in which he made three big hundreds. But then the rot set in.

On a gruelling tour of India and South Africa in 1969–70 the strain seemed to get to him. In India he repeatedly clashed with officials and the media, and in South Africa he added antagonising spectators into the mix. What is more, a non smoker and non drinker, he became more distant from his own team. 'He became a virtual recluse,' Jack Pollard wrote, 'disappearing after each day's play.'

His form with the bat was also less impressive, with only 432 runs at 28.80 in nine Tests on the tour.

It was on that trip that Lawry took on his own cricket board head on. Unhappy at a punishing itinerary and poor conditions, he adopted an increasingly confrontational approach. Lawry eventually wrote a letter to the board outlining the organisational faults of the tour, a move he admitted caused him 'a lot of strife'. He added: 'I think they took exception to that.'

'As far as I am concerned, putting in that letter was the

end of Lawry as captain,' Chappell said. 'Then it was just a matter of them getting rid of him.'

The 1970–71 Ashes started with Lawry still under a cloud after a scathing report by tour manager Fred Bennett. As the series progressed, Lawry came under fire for some uninspiring captaincy with a safety-at-all-costs strategy. In the fourth Test at Sydney, England went ahead with a 299-run win, and his critics became more vocal. His own batting, which was committed but never spectacular – Ian Wooldridge, the English journalist, called him 'a corpse with pads on' – had become even more stodgy. In the series he had batted more than 24 hours, averaging around 13 runs an hour.

In the fifth and sixth Tests Australia continued to lack enterprise. 'It has hardly been possible to find a taxi driver in the last couple of months who has not thought that Lawry should go,' wrote John Woodcock in *The Times*. At the end of the sixth Test, Keith Miller had called for the banishment of Lawry, Illingworth and the urn, so dire had the cricket become.

With a win needed in the deciding Test, Australia's selectors had no qualms about ditching an ultra-defensive leader who had also been a pain in their collective backsides. *Wisden* noted that 'he was negatively unimaginative but to drop him from the side for the vital last match was generous to England'.

'I've no anger about being dropped,' Lawry said. 'I hadn't been playing well in that series and I had no compassion when I was dropping players as a selector.'

As Lawry found out the news third-hand, Chappell was told of his appointment. 'It's unbelievable,' was his first reaction. 'I feel sorry for Bill ... he's been a good captain.' But knew what was in store, as he later recalled. 'I said to my wife, Kay, "The bastards will never get me like that".'

Paul Sheahan, another who had played under Lawry, was equally appalled at the manner the situation had been handled. 'The fact that no-one had the courage to tell him he was to lose his job as Australian captain was disgraceful.'

England won the final Test, and with it the series and the Ashes, and the Australian side, which contained three other uninspiring changes, was simply not good enough. Lawry, meanwhile, had already been signed up as a commentator; a career that lasts to this day.

And if the board thought that replacing Lawry with Chappell would make their life easier, they were soon given a rude wake-up call. Chappell, who had been instrumental in leading a player revolt against the side playing an extra Test in South Africa in 1970, was very much his own man, and he soon showed he was prepared to take them on, gloves off. The seeds of what ended in Kerry Packer's World Series Cricket had been sown.

SHIELD MATCH IS LAWRY'S LAST STAND

Today's Victoria v South Australia clash at the MCG to decide the Sheffield Shield sees six or seven borderline candidates making their last bid for the Australian side for England, which will be announced after the match. Most of the debate and the heat among cricket followers centres on former Australian captain Bill Lawry. Having been an automatic selection in every Australian XI since June 1961, Bill Lawry was dropped from the team and the captaincy last February and did not regain a place during the series against the Rest of the World. His supporters, and they are vocal in Victoria, say that on this year's performances he is, with teammate Keith Stackpole, head and shoulders above any other opener in Australia.

RIVAL IS SKIPPER

Lawry, 35 last month, has indicated that if his bid to regain his place fails, this will probably be his last appearance in first-class cricket.

— ROHAN RIVETT, *CANBERRA TIMES*, 3 MARCH 1972

NEILL PHILLIPSON

From The Australian Cricket Hall of Fame: Great cricketers past and present

Of all the Test players who have captained Australia it would be difficult to imagine one who has been more unjustly maligned than Bill Lawry. And yet it would be equally difficult to name one who had more ability. Bill Lawry's tragedy was that he lost the support of a section of the press, and thus the public, at a time when he needed it most.

Certainly when he was sacked from both the captaincy and the Australia side when a Test series was at its most critical stage, and sacked in a manner that was shameful in its execution, many cooler heads were shaken in dismay. Of all the batsmen available in Australia at that time he was perhaps the only one who could have salvaged the situation – and the Ashes.

The incredible thing about Bill Lawry was his ability to change his approach as the need dictated. As he grew older he became much more introspective about his game; unfortunately, and most of his critics tend to fall into this trap, the superficial aspects of his strokeplay tend to be remembered more than his brilliant knocks: his dour innings, most of which were played when Australia desperately needed a batsman who could dig in, take the edge off the attack and consolidate an innings. He was a player who developed almost perfect judgement and always adhered to the principle that the bowlers were there to get him out – if they could. He had a complete knowledge of his own limitations and did not believe in excesses at the batting crease, although he did have a weakness for the hook. Some of his more vehement

detractors tend to forget that many of his lengthy occupations of the crease were responsible for saving the day for Australia.

Less at home against spin than fast bowling, his batting was characterised by a short back lift and foot placement that left no room between bat and pad. It was this concentration of effort coupled with his absolute refusal to venture down the wicket in the face of spin which made him such a difficult batsman to dislodge.

When he replaced Bobby Simpson [as captain], whose premature retirement set the scene for Lawry's own removal four years later, Australia was entering the cricketing crossroads. For most of the matches he led the country, he was forced to rely on the sole efforts of Graham McKenzie to carry his pace attack. When McKenzie failed, as he did in South Africa, Lawry had little with which to cover the deficiency. It was ironical that it was in the series that cost him the captaincy that the backbone of the successful Chappell era, Dennis Lillee, made his debut. But for Bill Lawry, one of Australia's most dedicated and misunderstood captains, it was too late.

GREG CHAPPELL

I made my Test debut at the WACA under Bill's captaincy. Unfortunately, by that stage, politically, Bill's cards had been marked because he'd started the battle with the Australian Cricket Board over Australian cricketers' playing conditions and rights that my brother Ian and I would continue. A year earlier, Bill had led Australia on back-to-back Test tours of India and South Africa.

On the field, the tour of India went very well with Australia winning the five Test series 3-1, the last time that we would win a Test series in India for nearly 35 years. Off the field, the Australian players were left wondering why, despite the presence of excellent hotels in India, the Board was putting them up in sub-standard accommodation.

By the end of that gruelling two month tour of India, which featured five Tests and five first-class matches, the Australians were knackered. But the Board sent them straight on to South Africa for a four Test series against a South African team boasting Barry Richards, Graeme Pollock and Mike Procter that many rated the best in the world. The exhausted Australians were duly smashed 4-0. Towards the end of the tour, the Board, without consulting the Australian players, scheduled an extra game. The players had had enough and refused to play it.

A team meeting was held and a letter was drafted setting out the players' complaints about the way that they were being treated by the Board. The players were happy to sign the letter as a team, but Bill said: 'No, I'm captain. It's my responsibility. I'll sign it.' Bill sent the letter off to the Board with himself as the sole signatory

and I've always believed that that played a big part in his eventual demise as Australian captain.

From that point on, the Board was just looking for a reason to sack him and they duly got it in the home Ashes summer of 1970–71 when Australia, 1–0 down in a seven Test series, drew the sixth Test to foreclose any possibility of an Australian series victory. Bill was summarily sacked as Australian captain and dropped from the Australian Test XI. He'd never play Test cricket again.

Thus, I wasn't able to get to know him well during his playing days. His Test career ended just as mine was beginning. In the four Tests that I played with him in that home Ashes summer of 1970–71, we didn't get the chance to speak much. I saw him at the ground and that was about it. He didn't drink, so I didn't see him much socially after the day's play. It was clear that he took his cricket and his responsibilities as Australian captain seriously and that he was a fierce competitor who played with his heart and soul every time he stepped out onto the field. But he seemed, to my 22-year-old self, to be a pretty austere sort of fellow.

You see a situation and say to yourself, 'I am going to be here at stumps'. That's part of your job. It's all very well to be flamboyant, but if you get beat, that's not a lot of fun.
— Bill Lawry

TOM RYAN

I only played three games alongside Bill Lawry during the 1965–66 season and his appearances for Northcote over the following years were few, especially after he was appointed Australia's 32nd Test captain in January, 1968. For me, though, it was time enough to discover a very different Phantom from the one who'd piled on the centuries in that Greensborough garage. This Phantom was a flesh-and-blood human being and as I got to know him better, my sense of awe merged with a fuller appreciation of what made him tick.

He was an inspiring leader: where he led, you'd follow. He'd never ask you to do something that he wasn't prepared to do himself. Actually, come to think of it, that's not quite true. There was that time I was bold enough to ask why he'd sent me in as a nightwatchman opener when we had to bat for 20 minutes in fading light before stumps. After all, I reasoned, he was the opening batsman for Australia; I was just a kid trying to make some runs at club level. His response was to the point: 'Do you want to win the game or not?'

He was – and still is – a perceptive reader of the rhythms of a game. He was the kind of batsman and captain who'd adapt his approach to an innings or a match according to what he saw as the demands of the day. He was a gritty fighter who'd never surrender. The English journalist Ian Wooldridge famously labelled him the 'corpse with pads on' after watching him labour five-and-a-quarter hours to score 94 at The Oval in 1964. But the truth is: Bill could blaze with the best of them, if the situation required or allowed. What people tend to forget

is that that glacial 94 at The Oval in 1964 was exactly what his team required: Australia held a 1–0 series lead and only needed to draw that final Test at The Oval to win the series.

He was also a mischievous scallywag who'd affectionately take the piss out of teammates and opponents alike. One day, sometime in the 1970s, I was walking past the Star – Melbourne's first pornographic theatre – on Elizabeth Street when I happened to run into Phanta. 'Aha, gotcha!' he exclaimed, as if he'd caught me with my pants down. For him, at least, it became a hilarious running joke, especially since I went on to teach film at university and become a professional film critic.

As a leader, he dispensed praise sparingly, and he made sure you stayed grounded. At a dinner soon after the Grand Final, he announced to the gathered dignitaries that I'd batted well, adding that 'maybe now Tommy can stop talking about runs and start making some!' (For some reason, I've always been 'Tommy' to anyone I've played cricket with or against.)

On the field, he expected you to do the job that you'd been picked to do. If your shot selection was careless, he'd let you know but he wouldn't shout at you. The worst I ever heard from the abundant opportunities that I provided for him was 'Jeez, Tommy!' That was enough to point out that you'd let him, the team and yourself down. He captained by example, and his wit and sense of humour came in handy too. Once, our fearsome opening bowler, Rodney Hogg, later to become a Test great, dropped an absolute sitter at mid-on off my bowling. Phanta was fielding at mid-off. I saw Hoggy quaking in his sprigged boots, waiting for the spray that most captains would deliver in such a situation. Instead, Phanta just raised an eyebrow at him and said, 'Well, at least you stopped it.'

He always had a plan for opposing batsmen. He mightn't have been much chop as a bowler, but he knew what he wanted from those he called upon to take wickets. And he'd use fieldsmen like a puppeteer. I remember him quietly explaining to me how we were going to trick Paul Sheahan into taking a short single that wasn't there. 'Yeah, right!' I thought to myself. But I did as I was told and, within a couple of overs, it had worked. He truly was a maestro when it came to conducting the field of play.

If he had a flaw, it was one that was later to become a professional strength. Whenever he became an off-field observer, his engagement with the match unfolding on the field was always palpable. To sit within earshot of him, let alone alongside him, while waiting to bat was a deeply unnerving experience. Long before he graced Channel 9's commentary team, it was all happening whenever Bill watched a match from the sheds. 'He's out!' he'd yell, jumping to his feet. More often than not, the batsman wasn't out at all. But by the time he was, you'd stagger on to the field a nervous wreck. I'm still reminded of this every time he fronts up for his turn at the microphone during a Test match. And my wife wonders what I'm on about when I tell her, after a long day on the couch listening to him, that I'm totally wrung out. Now that's what I call PTSD.

I run into him from time to time at Northcote matches and club reunions. He'll bounce up with a chirpy 'Tommy Ryan!' and I'll still find it hard to believe that, for a short time in the 1960s and '70s, I played alongside an Australian cricket legend. It was a privilege that I've never forgotten. And if you're standing in the vicinity, you might even hear me saying 'How's zat?' to the cricket-loving kid still lingering somewhere inside.

In conjunction with the Northcote Cricket Club the Victorian Cricket Association renamed Northcote Park the Bill Lawry Oval. This is perhaps the most appropriate recognition of a humble cricketer who should be feted for his sterling performances on the field, his loyalty to his teammates, and his great love of all things Victorian.
— Stuart Wark, ESPN

COMMENTATOR

NINE NETWORK COMMENTATOR BILL LAWRY
AT THE SYDNEY CRICKET GROUND IN 2004.
(PHOTO BY HAMISH BLAIR/GETTY IMAGES)

BILL LAWRY

Interviewed by Sidharth Monga

I first got into commentary when we were playing state one-day games. There were Richie Benaud, myself and Bobby Simpson, working for Channel 10. Channel 0 [it was called] back then. We did one or two of those, on small grounds. And then, of course, along comes Kerry Packer in 1977–78, and the first commentary team was Richie Benaud, Fred Trueman, Keith Stackpole, and myself.

I was an estate manager for a manufacturing company and had a full-time job. This just came along. Something new. Under lights, coloured clothing. We had a great time.

Keith Stackpole and I had never done television over a long period before, and Frank Tyson joined the team as well. And we had guest commentators over the years come from every country.

Richie had been commentating in England since 1960–61, so we had his experience.

It was all new. Everybody was excited. We had cameras at both ends for the first time in the history of the game. We had cameras square of the wicket. We had all these wonderful new things. Exciting time. Very lucky to be there.

And of course we had very good players. Australia had the Chappell brothers and Lillee and Marsh, and all these types of guys. The World XI was Tony Greig, and West Indies with Clive Lloyd, and all their wonderful cricketers. It was just an exciting time. Changing of the guard as far as cricket was concerned. All of a sudden we had an outside promoter promoting the game rather than the cricket boards.

Once Kerry Packer came along, it became a professional sport. What we see today, 40 years on, what we take for granted, all started with World Series Cricket. He paid the players well, the crowds were big, we went full-time on television. We had no instructions whatsoever.

It was not a career for me. Until I retired at 65 I did [it] for fun. I got a pay obviously, but I did it for fun. Just an add-on to my working career. It's just been a wonderful enjoyment. I enjoy the money – because I never got any money when I played – but I have enjoyed more the thrill of watching great players over the years. The Vivian Richardses, the Lillees, the Chappell brothers, the Bothams [then] the Pontings and the Shane Warnes...

Our first producer was a guy called David Hill. And he just said, 'Be yourself.' That's all. I just come along to enjoy the cricket, and hopefully convey to the people at home that I am enjoying the cricket, and it's a great game, and I enjoy the skill. I mean, how fortunate are we to be sitting right behind the wicket?

KEITH STACKPOLE

We were reunited as teammates when Kerry Packer chose us to be commentators for World Series Cricket. We formed part of the inaugural four-man commentary team for the first Super Test at Waverley Park in Melbourne's outer south-eastern suburbs. Richie Benaud of course was our captain and Fred Trueman was the fourth member of our team. Tony Cozier joined us after the first Super Test to make it a five-man team.

Those early years of World Series Cricket would turn out to be some of the most exciting years of our lives. It was thrilling and fascinating to be involved with such an ambitious, innovative venture at the ground level. Channel 9 was a magnificent employer and David Hill, our producer, was a genius. Kerry Packer was deeply involved in the enterprise from the very beginning, often taking a hands-on approach.

In the early days, we faced a lot of resistance and criticism from viewers who were used to the ABC's TV coverage. The ABC only had a camera at one end, so, every second over, the viewer had to watch the game from directly behind the keeper. All the viewer could see was the keeper's backside. One of the most basic innovations that World Series Cricket introduced was having a camera behind the bowler at both ends. Believe it or not, people complained to Channel 9 about this! I guess they liked looking at keepers' backsides.

The ABC's commentary style was very dry and matter-of-fact, not much different from a newsreader. What we started off, I think all of us, Bill included, probably felt a bit constrained by that traditional style of commentary. But Kerry wanted something completely different from us. 'I want you to really tell the story of what is happening out there', he said. 'Tell people what the players out there are feeling and thinking. And take risks – tell people what you would do if you were in the position of the batsman, bowler or fielding captain.'

Kerry loved Bill, because his voice was different. After an early one-day game in which Bill allowed some of his decidedly non-ABC-style enthusiasm to show through, Kerry told him: 'That was great. I don't want you to be like the ABC. I want you to be like yourself. Just call it as you see it.' Over time, Bill became more and more confident in being himself on the air, and developed into the commentator that we all know and love today.

Kerry wanted us to take risks and nobody took more risks than Bill. As a commentator, you can either commentate off the actual action out on the field or a live TV monitor that Channel 9 has in the commentary box. Plenty of commentators work off the latter, because it ensures that they never make a mistake. Not Bill. He always commentates off the on-field action. He's spontaneous. He calls it as he sees it and makes the viewers feel as if they're out there in the middle with him.

GREG CHAPPELL

When I retired from Test cricket and joined the Channel 9 commentary team, I discovered that Bill was anything but austere. He's a gregarious bloke, a real joker with a wonderful, dry sense of humour. I'm reliably informed that that's what he was like in his early days in the Australian team, before he was weighed down by the burden of the Australian captaincy.

During my years as Channel 9 commentator, every morning, Bill would be the first to arrive in the box. He would sit there and watch everything that happened leading up to the start of play. Whenever he was commentating, he would sit on the edge of his chair, like a kid watching his favourite movie. The enthusiasm that you hear in his voice is real. If anything dramatic happened on the field, he would leap into the air in the commentary box. He was more overtly emotionally involved in the game than any other cricket commentator I've worked with.

Bill's sheer enthusiasm could sometimes pose a challenge to his co-commentator. When a Channel 9 commentator wants to speak on air, he has to pick up his lip ribbon microphone – essentially, a mic mounted on top of a pole about the height of a pint glass – and hold it very close to his mouth. When the commentator finishes speaking, he places his lip ribbon microphone down on the table in front of him. Then, if his co-commentator wishes to speak, he picks up his lip ribbon microphone.

This process confers two advantages. Firstly, hardly any background noise goes to air, because when the lip ribbon microphones are placed down on the table, they don't pick up much noise at all. Secondly, broadcasting's cardinal sin of commentators talking over each other is avoided, because each commentator can easily see whether his co-commentator has picked up his lip ribbon microphone.

Every Channel 9 commentator I worked with put his microphone down once he'd finished speaking, except for Bill. He never put his microphone down! So when you were commentating with Bill, you had to constantly keep one eye on him to see when he'd finished speaking or just wait for him to take a breath then jump in. Otherwise, you didn't get much of a say.

The other unique thing about Bill as a co-commentator was that, as soon as you started speaking, he'd turn towards you with his microphone still held up to his mouth and look intently at you as you spoke, waiting for you to finish so that he could say something. I must admit that, when I first started as a commentator, I found this to be a little off-putting. But I soon worked out how to co-commentate effectively with Bill. Firstly, when he was speaking, I had to watch him intently

to know when I could jump in. Secondly, as soon as I started talking, I had to turn away from him, so that I couldn't see him peering at me over his distinctive beak, almost willing me to put the microphone down.

Co-commentating with Bill was a thoroughly enjoyable, albeit slightly challenging experience!

The funniest incident that I witnessed with Bill as a Channel 9 commentator took place at Bellerive Oval in early February 1993. Tasmania were playing Queensland in a 50-over Mercantile Mutual Cup game and Channel 9 brought down the full commentary team. Back in those days, the commentary boxes at Bellerive were nothing more than two shipping container boxes perched on top of some big scaffolding down the southern end of the ground. As you can imagine, there wasn't much room in the commentary box. When we weren't on air, all of us commentators – except for Richie Benaud, who had his own studio where Channel 9 recorded his before play introductions and end of day's play summaries – had to crowd up the back of the box.

We were there, watching from the back of the box, when Richie and Bill went on air at the start of Tasmania's innings. Bill was in the driver's seat, doing the ball-by-ball commentary, while Richie was sitting happily in the special comments seat. When they were co-commentating together, Richie was generally very happy to just let Bill go. He knew that he didn't have to say too much, because Bill was going to say plenty. By this point, Billy Birmingham had been doing his *The Twelfth Man* parody for years. All of us Channel 9 commentators were well aware of *The Twelfth Man* and joked about it, except when Richie was around.

Pretty soon, Tasmania reach 2/22 and Bill says, 'tchew for tchewenty-two.' Then, for the first time in his career as a commentator, he puts the microphone down and starts laughing. Richie just sits in his chair, looking at Bill impassively. Meanwhile, Bill just keeps laughing. Every time he stops, he looks up, sees Richie looking down his lip at him and starts laughing again. So two-and-a-half overs of the match go by without any commentary. Bill can't commentate and Richie won't.

Up the back of the box, we're pissing ourselves laughing. It was just so typical of Richie and Bill. It was sensational.

IAN CHAPPELL, BILL LAWRY, BOB SIMPSON AND RICHIE BENAUD IN MELBOURNE, 20 SEPTEMBER 1977. (FAIRFAX)

I have been one of the lucky generation, to have gone on from being an amateur to a professional on television but not as a career, as a hobby and a delight.
— *Bill Lawry*

Having known Bill for some 58 years, I can tell you that what you see is what you get. He's a passionate Victorian and a good friend. He's a down-to-earth bloke who loves his family, cricket, pigeons and baseball.
— *Keith Stackpole*

Interestingly, *The Twelfth Man* played a vital role in helping Bill become the infectiously enthusiastic commentator that we all know and love today. When Bill first started at Channel 9 as a commentator during World Series Cricket, his commentary style was that of the bog standard ABC commentator: as dour as his batting in the latter stages of his Test career. Keep in mind that, when World Series Cricket started in early December 1977, the matter-of-fact ABC commentary style was all any of us knew.

Over time, Bill started becoming more like himself, but what tipped him over the edge was the release of the first *The Twelfth Man* single in 1984. Bill thought that *The Twelfth Man*'s parody of him was hilarious. More importantly, the wide scale public release and commercial success of the parody liberated him. He was finally free to just be himself on-air and, from that point on, that's exactly what he's done.

As funny and entertaining as Bill is on-air, that's nothing compared with him as an after dinner speaker. When I was back in Adelaide coaching South Australia between 1998 and 2003, I became a patron of the Leukaemia Foundation of South Australia. One of my tasks was to arrange a dinner each year to raise funds for the foundation. Every year, I got two or three cricket personalities as our after dinner speakers and put them up on stage on a panel. One year, I got Bill and Bob Simpson for our dinner at Adelaide Oval and it was sensational. Bill took the piss out of himself and took the piss out of Bobby Simpson mercilessly. It was all very self-deprecating, very dry humour and the audience absolutely loved it! It was totally at odds with what most people, even with his commentary, expect of him. Until that evening, I hadn't fully seen that side of Bill either.

From that time onwards, whenever people asked me who I'd recommend as an after dinner speak, I always replied: 'get Bill Lawry.' A lot of people were sceptical, but I'd always say, 'trust me, he is one of the funniest blokes going around.' And every time, people would get back in touch with me after their dinner and say, 'thanks very much, Bill was fantastic!'

Richie was my first Test captain, and he was a very good cricket captain, but he has been an exceptional captain of the Channel Nine team. He has set the standard. He gave us credibility, and his knowledge of the game was fantastic. Blokes like myself were allowed to be a bit vocal because he was the steady influence on the other side of the mic. You could always look up and see Richie was there and feel safe.

— Bill Lawry

THE 1993 CHANNEL NINE CRICKET COMMENTARY TEAM (FROM LEFT) GREG CHAPPELL, IAN CHAPPELL, RICHIE BENAUD, BILL LAWRY AND TONY GREIG, ALL FORMER TEST CAPTAINS. (FAIRFAX)

BILL LAWRY AND TONY GREIG.
(GETTY IMAGES)

MAX KRUGER

From *Tony Greig: Love, War and Cricket*

There was the rock-solid opening batsman – serious yet excitable. Then there was the brash all-rounder who loved to engage the crowd and who was happy to be portrayed as the villain. Different people but united by a love of the great game. The rapport developed over time. Cricket at Test level stretches over five days. That is a long time to be around each other in the confines of the commentary box. It was clear that they enjoyed working together. Bill would go with the moment. If Tony disagreed, he would say so. This would invoke an exchange of views. Who would win? Bill thrived on the right of veto – the final word. It really depended on who was the lead commentator, that is, who led the call and, significantly, who would throw to the commercial break.

This would result in vigorous debate in the break. Back on air and the lead man would pick up the call. Depending on what had triggered the discussion in the first place, it may be left there or it could be the catalyst for round two, for it is fair to say that both men liked to have the final word. It was fun to be around when something controversial happened on their watch. Tony loved to stir the pot. Just as he did in his playing days, he liked to keep people on their toes. And Bill had his agenda items. Tony knew he would always get an immediate reaction if he criticised one of Bill's beloved fellow Victorians.

Both relished the opportunity to commentate when the game had hit a flat spot; it seemed they had the power to make something happen out of nowhere. You sensed they both had their checklists – the topics that would always get a reaction. Sitting alongside them, this was how I thought they would assess each other and find the points that would create a conversation.

There was Eastern-Suburbs Tony: posh school education; mercenary cricketer and company man; career commentator; former England captain; shared allegiances between South Africa, England and Sri Lanka; and probably the one that irritated Bill the most – proud Sydney-ite.

Alongside that was Blue-Collar Bill: state school education; plumber by trade; pigeon fancier; part-time commentator; former Australian captain; parochial Victorian.

Tony enjoyed highlighting that Bill was the skipper when Australia was thrashed four–nil by South Africa in 1970. If someone started batting slowly, Bill's career resume would need to be revisited. A close-up on a pigeon was always well received by Tony.

Bill would love to talk about the real people – the battlers. To him, they were a world away from Greig's cushy existence. And didn't Bill just love it when Tony commented on the attractiveness of a lovely young lady in the crowd.

It seemed uncanny how often a wicket would fall soon after Bill took over the call. Tony would feed off this and another memorable stint would be underway.

There was an innate competitiveness between them, but what unified them was the shared desire to entertain. Many a time Tony would say, 'Come on, Bill, let's stir it up.' Tony would look at me and ask me to give them something to bring it alive. I don't know why he would say that because, as sure as night followed day, something would always happen as soon as they took up the call.

Boxing Day Tests in Melbourne have been a tradition for most of the Channel Nine era. Who could ever forget Tony Greig's dramatic call of the final ball when Dennis Lillee knocked over Viv Richards to have the mighty West Indies reeling at 4–10 at stumps on Boxing Day 1981? Tony loved the big stage but Bill would always remind him, 'This is the sporting capital of Australia,' when he was feeling subdued. When he was on a roll, Melbourne was elevated to the 'sporting capital of the world'. No false modesty from Bill.

This was Bill's playground. He would be eager to talk about the big occasion; the size and the passion of the crowd; and all things Victorian. However, there was a key variable – Melbourne's fickle weather. Rain interruptions were perfect fodder for Tony. Many of the first days were rain-affected.

Then another New Year would come around and Sydney would play host to its annual New Year's Test. I'm sure Tony would hold his breath and hope for favourable weather. If rain was in the air, Bill was ready to pounce.

Tony would wax lyrical about Sydney. He would have his fun and then seek a concession from Bill that this was indeed God's own country. Bill would be most likely to say: 'Okay, Tony Greig, you've had your fun. Let's get back to the cricket.'

The Centennary Match at Lord's, captains of England and Australia. (left to right) Bob Wyatt, Lindsay Hassett, Gubby Allen, Cyril Walters, Arthur Morris, Norman Yardley, Freddie Brown, Richie Benaud, Sir Leonard Hutton, Neil Harvey, Peter May, Bob Simpson, Bill Lawry, Ted Dexter, Mike Smith, Barry Jarman, Tom Graveney, Ian Chappell, Graham Yallop, Greg Chappell and Ian Botham.
(PA IMAGES VIA GETTY IMAGES)

Lawry became a popular TV commentator on Channel Nine. He wasn't able to emulate United States President Ronald Reagan by making clichés sound original, but his familiar, repetitive comments – 'There's a good crowd in' – and shrill cries – 'Got 'im! Yes!' and 'It's all happening!' – amused but didn't offend the vast TV audience. He was even the subject of mimicry by comedians, a sure sign that he was a national 'household name'.

— Roland Perry

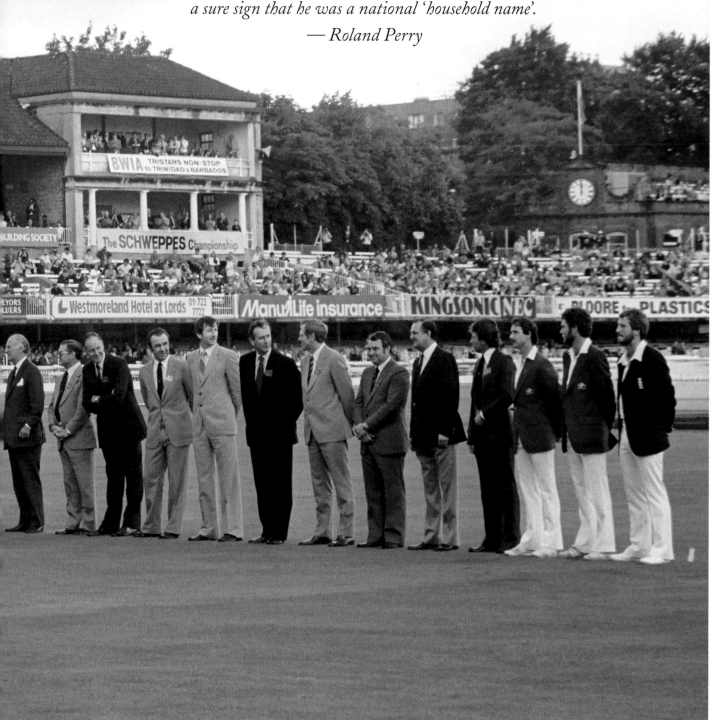

IAN HEALY

Growing up in the outback town of Biloela in central Queensland in the 1970s, the Australian Test openers who I watched on TV and heard on radio were Ian Redpath and Keith Stackpole. Their fellow Victorian and former Australian captain, Bill Lawry, had just finished his Test career, so I never got to watch him. I heard about him though. He was reputed to be a dour and resolute batsman, an opener who put the highest possible price on his wicket, but also sometimes put the crowd to sleep! Of course, I later learned that that reputation wasn't entirely accurate. When his team needed quick runs, he could entertain with the best of them.

I first met Bill when we played Victoria in a Shield game at the Junction Oval in late November 1992. I'd just been appointed captain of Queensland and Bill was Victoria's cricket manager, so we said g'day. He was very down to earth. There were no airs or graces about him. I remember thinking how good it was to see a legendary former Australian captain like Bill choose to contribute to the modern game by taking on the cricket manager role. After all, he didn't have to do that job: he was already gainfully employed – and nationally renowned – as a Channel 9 cricket commentator.

It would be another seven years before I got the chance to really get to know Bill. During my Test career, we weren't able to interact much. It wasn't like it is now where the Channel 9 commentators are frequently out on the ground interviewing the players and sometimes even going into the dressing room TV cameras in tow. Back then, the Channel 9 commentators just stayed in their commentary box. If any of us players wanted to get to know the Channel 9 commentators better, we'd have

to arrange to have dinner with them. I distinctly recall Warnie and I having dinner with Richie Benaud once, but I don't think I ever had dinner with Bill when I was still playing for Australia.

After I retired from Test cricket in late 1999, I moved into the Channel 9 commentary box. Since then, I've gotten to know Bill very well. We've become good mates and I've learnt a heck of a lot about the art of commentating just by watching him go about his work. As Test cricketers, we're trained to watch quietly in the dressing room, so as to not disturb the emotional equilibrium of the team. That is especially important when a batsman's just gotten out or the game has reached a critical, pressure-packed juncture. The aim is always to avoid emotional rollercoasters and keep the team's emotional equilibrium nice and level.

But once you become a Channel 9 commentator, your job is to take the viewers at home on the rollercoaster as the game ebbs and flows. Nobody does that better than Bill. He has the ability to excite people with his commentary, because he himself is still genuinely excited to be watching cricket day in, day out. I still remember my very first day as a Channel 9 commentator, day one of the 1999 Gabba Test against Pakistan. I got there nice and early, thinking that I'd be the first commentator to arrive for work that morning, and discovered Bill, already sitting in his chair in the commentary box. He still does that every day he commentates on the cricket for Channel Nine.

Bill understands that life – and cricket – are supposed to be fun. He has the ability to look at things with a sense of humour. He's also a model professional. He's always thinking cricket and he always does his homework on players. He doesn't get distracted by Facebook, Twitter, Instagram, Snapchat, emails or texts. He just sits there all day, contently watching every ball bowled. Like any great Test cricketer, his job performance is as good at the end of the day as it is at the start of the day.

There's nothing better than co-commentating with Bill. He's always infectious with excitement and saying plenty, giving you lots of stuff to either agree or disagree with and discuss and debate. It's excellent working with him. He's got a wonderful natural ability to tell yarns. He puts that ability to good use off air too, telling us funny stories about his days on tour.

His legendary opening partnership with Bobby Simpson is one of his favourite subjects to take the piss out of. 'C'mon, let's entertain them today,' said Simmo one day as they were walking out to bat for Australia. 'Aw, entertain them,' replied Bill, 'for two and sixpence, piss off! I'm just staying in.' Then there was their exceptional running between the wickets – they were quick, pinching every single available and constantly rotating the strike. Of course, that meant that there was the occasional mix-up, which Bill still enjoys teasing Simmo about: 'Get ready, whether he's on 0, 49 or 99, get ready, he'll run you out!'

I look forward to many more years of Bill's company.

He makes work fun. There's a general joy around the commentary box whenever he's there. And that joy envelops not just the commentators, but the crew too. They love having him around.
— Ian Healy

BILL LAWRY AND IAN HEALY COMMENTATE DURING DAY FIVE OF THE FOURTH TEST MATCH IN THE ASHES SERIES BETWEEN AUSTRALIA AND ENGLAND AT THE MELBOURNE CRICKET GROUND IN 2017. (SCOTT BARBOUR/GETTY IMAGES)

BILL LAWRY

Interviewed by Sidharth Monga

I was always excitable when I played. It might not have shown in my batting, but I always appealed the loudest in the field. In fact when I was on my first tour of England, I was fielding at square leg or somewhere, and I came in after the game, and Mr Jack Fingleton [then a journalist] called me aside and said, 'Bill it's great to be enthusiastic, but you shouldn't be appealing for lbws at deep midwicket'.

I just try and call each ball as I see it. I love to get a wicket, I love to get a great catch or a run-out. I just try and be involved without going over the top.

You have got to make sure when you get those wickets, that everybody at home – if he is outside in the garden – comes in to see what is going on. You want him to say, 'What was that noise?' and go in and see a wicket has fallen.

I don't try and analyse it too much. I just try and bring in my experiences as a player. I realise that probably 70% of the people at home are not cricket experts. I try and explain it to them. When we first started, David Hill actually had a chart up on the wall with field positions, because when we were saying to somebody who has migrated to Australia, 'He has got a man at leg gully', what does leg gully mean to a 14-year-old girl or a young boy who is not brought up in a cricketing family? What is silly point? A traffic stop or something?

I always watch. I don't bring a computer to the ground. I don't do any other work at all. I just watch the game. That was because David Hill earlier on said that if you are on next, I don't want you to repeat what the guy before said. Most times I sit in there, I watch what's going on, so when I am on, I have got my thoughts, not Richie Benaud's or Tony Greig's. And I love watching the cricket, and I have always loved watching it, and I think you can learn by watching.

Richie Benaud is a man of few words. He is an analyst. He analyses the game. Tony Greig talks about Africa. He cares about Africa. All that sort of stuff. I bring out my feelings about the game. Luckily there have been very few changes. You don't have a 30-year career as a cricketer.

NINE COMMENTARY TEAM MEMBERS (LEFT TO RIGHT) MICHAEL
CLARKE, IAN HEALY, SHANE WARNE, MARK NICHOLAS, BILL
LAWRY, MICHAEL SLATER AND MARK TAYLOR POSE FOR A SELFIE
IN THEIR MJ BALE PINK JACKETS IN SUPPORT OF MCGRATH PINK
TEST DURING DAY THREE OF THE FIFTH TEST MATCH IN THE
2017–18 ASHES SERIES BETWEEN AUSTRALIA AND ENGLAND AT
SYDNEY CRICKET GROUND ON 6 JANUARY 2018,
(RYAN PIERSE/GETTY IMAGES)

CHANNEL 9 COMMENTATORS
IAN HEALY, RICHIE BENAUD,
MICHAEL SLATER, BRETT
LEE, IAN CHAPPELL AND BILL
LAWRY ON THE GROUND
DURING A TEA BREAK OF THE
THIRD TEST MATCH BETWEEN
AUSTRALIA AND SRI LANKA AT
THE SYDNEY CRICKET GROUND
IN 2013. (MARK KOLBE/GETTY
IMAGES)

ANTHONY SHARWOOD

No Bill Lawry, it's just not cricket

No one, not even the master mimic, can pull off an exaggerated Bill Lawry impersonation, and that's because Bill leaves them no room to work with.

Fact is, a summer without Lawry is like a crowd without cheering.

When the first Twelfth Man soundtrack came out, Billy Birmingham's brilliant impersonations captured everyone in the Nine box perfectly. But while most of Birmingham's impersonations have always had an air of exaggerated pisstake, his Bill Lawry always sounded exactly like well, exactly like the real Bill Lawry.

No one, not even the master mimic, can pull off an exaggerated Bill Lawry impersonation, and that's because Bill leaves them no room to work with. Instead of curbing his own excitement, Bill works with it. He takes his emotions and rides them.

Bill doesn't do fake. By contrast, the new breed of commentators curb their emotions, lest anyone suspect they actually have a personality.

They also avoid criticising players, protecting both their former dressing room mates and their carefully-polished veneer of niceness, which has been honed by months of intensive media training.

OK, so Bill isn't always accurate. And occasionally, you might call him biased, especially on matters pertaining to persons hailing from south of the Murray River and north of Bass Strait.

But by God, he's fun to listen to. Somewhere along the way, plenty of people in the sports media forget that sport is supposed to be fun. You can feel Bill enjoying himself at work. And because he's having a good time, you do too.

Richie Benaud once famously said something to the effect that the art of TV commentary is not to comment on what the viewer can see for themselves.

Wise words, but they don't hold true for Bill. The art of Lawry is his ability to tell us what we can all see for ourselves, really, really loudly.

Technically, it shouldn't work. But it does. It just does.

I've known the Phantom for 66 years and I can tell you that he hasn't changed a bit. He enjoyed taking the mick out of us when he was 15 and he enjoys taking the mick out of us now. He was down at the club before Christmas doing just that. It was brilliant.
— *Barry Morrison*

Bill Lawry can get excited at the drop of a hat – by a shot, a ball, a catch. His job, he says, is to make the man in the garden come into the house to check what happened

A lot of commentary today is noise. Just gratuitous and grating shouting. Yet one of the most loved commentators of all time is a shouter. Like the rest today, Bill Lawry too is a peddler, but he sells enjoyment of the cricket. Talking to him, you understand why his loudness doesn't jar.
— *Sidharth Monga*

NINE COMMENTARY TEAM MEMBERS (LEFT TO RIGHT) MICHAEL CLARKE, IAN HEALY, IAN CHAPPELL, MARK NICHOLAS, BILL LAWRY, MICHAEL SLATER, MARK TAYLOR AND SHANE WARNE DURING THE FIFTH TEST MATCH IN THE ASHES SERIES BETWEEN AUSTRALIA AND ENGLAND AT SYDNEY CRICKET GROUND IN 2018. (RYAN PIERSE/GETTY IMAGES)

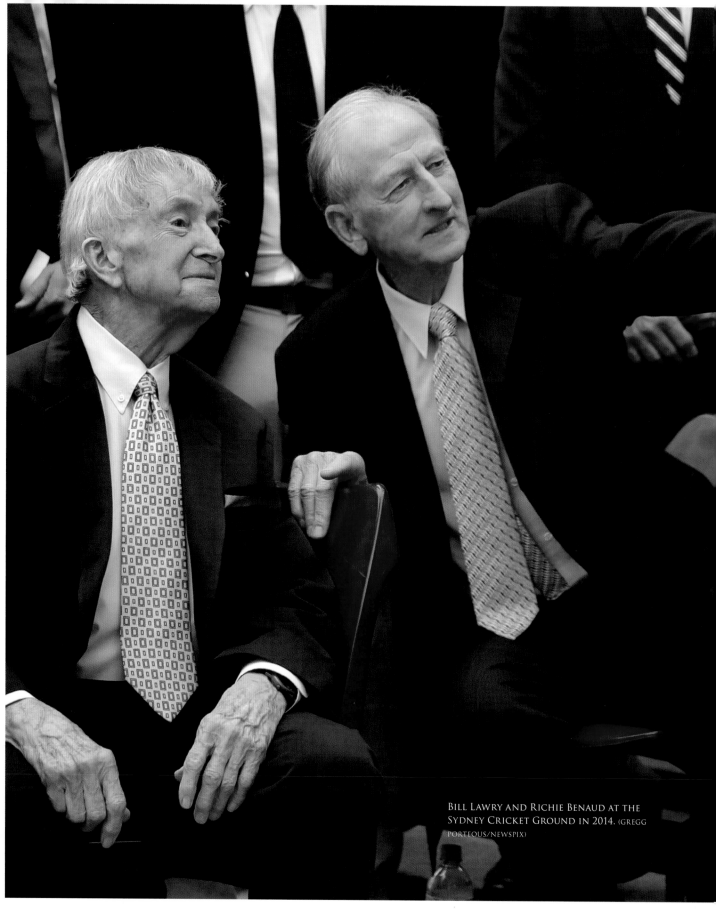

BILL LAWRY AND RICHIE BENAUD AT THE
SYDNEY CRICKET GROUND IN 2014. (GREGG
PORTEOUS/NEWSPIX)

TRENT DALTON

Call of the Wild

For the 33 summers of Channel Nine cricket commentary they shared, when they were commentating on games in venues outside Melbourne and Sydney, Tony Greig, Richie Benaud and Bill Lawry travelled together. Greig seemingly knew the shortest route to every major cricket ground across the world and, as such, insisted on taking the wheel. Bill took the front passenger seat. 'If Richie was with us I'd always get out of the front and hop in the back,' he says. 'You hop out for Richie.'

'Good morning,' Benaud would say, sliding into the front passenger seat with matinée idol elegance. And from the pocket of his beige-coloured sports coat he would produce a piece of paper with several handwritten names of touring cricketers from the Indian subcontinent.

'Righto, Bill,' he would say. 'Let's go through these names.'

'And he'd go through this list of names I hadn't pronounced correctly,' Bill says.

'Say it after me, Bill. Suu-neel Gav-as-kar.'

'Say it just like this, Bill. Mu-tti-ah Mura-lit-haran.'

'And I'd sort of mumble something back,' Bill says.

'WRONG!' Richie would say. 'Wrong, Bill, try again.'

'By the time I got to the ground I was a mumbling mess. Of course, the others didn't fall for it, they'd studied the names to avoid the same treatment. I never studied the names. He loved doing that to me. Richie would terrorise me with the pronunciations.'

Long may we measure the depth of Richie Benaud's character by Bill Lawry's seamless, note-perfect pronunciation of Shanthakumaran Sreesanth.

Long-time commentary colleague Ian Chappell is forever pulling people up at lunches, reminding them how few times he outscored William Morris Lawry in a game. Watch the old black-and-white footage and the textbook defence is there, the towering body that could loom over a short-pitched delivery like a shadow, the hawk nose that could sniff out the leather on a swirling off-cutter. But so, too, is a slashing grace. Bill Lawry could punch a straight drive the way Walter Lindrum struck a cue ball. His cut shot was a French guillotine that left British heads spinning. Benaud, as he was wont to do, had the last word on the matter of Bill's skill at the crease. 'One of the best batsmen ever to play for Australia,' he said.

ROB BAGCHI

Bill Lawry – the voice of Australian summers

If playing was the sum of Lawry's contribution to cricket, he would still be treasured by his teammates and those deviant souls who fetishise the sound of dead bat on ball and venerate the artful leave. But it is his career since joining the Channel 9 commentary team for the launch of World Series Cricket in 1977, which has been prolonged by post-retirement cameo appearances for the Boxing Day Test, that has made him an indelible part of Australian summers.

Of several British winters, too, beginning with the reconciliation, non-Ashes series of 1979–80 when the BBC first carried the coverage of the 'famous five': Richie Benaud, Ian Chappell, Tony Greig, Max Walker and Lawry. Benaud, mercifully, was always with us but for the years between tours of Australia, their characters, idiosyncrasies and fictional, peppery relationships with each other were burnished by bootleg copies of The 12th Man.

The genuine Lawry has been the most singular and vivid voice in cricket TV broadcasting of the past four decades, and his 'Yes, got 'im', 'It's all happening at the SCG', 'Bang, bang, bang', 'Neck and crop', 'Ripper', 'On your bike' and 'You beauty' have become part of the fabric of Australian broadcasting.

They are memorable as catchphrases, not for their insight. There is none of the lyrical charm of a John Arlott but there is no blather – Lawry has a gift for

articulating the immediate gut reaction of the most engaged spectator. He calls the game rather than instantly reflecting on what he has seen.

Over here he was misjudged as one-eyed while Australia were humiliating England on five successive tours, but looking back it sounds more like disappointment at the inadequacies of the tourists' technique and temperament. In 2010–11, far from being mortified by England's dominance, he revelled in the fine cricket they played and was more than magnanimous in his praise.

Lawry's strident, nasal Victorian tones can be clanging to the English ear, unlike the treacly Queensland resonance of the late Len Martin, the BBC's football results announcer for many years, or Benaud's wry Sydneysider cadences. As a player he was held responsible for almost killing the game, but as a commentator, his irrepressible, infectious enthusiasm has only enriched it.

BILL LAWRY PRESENTS
JOE BURNS HIS CAP AT
THE THIRD TEST MATCH
BETWEEN AUSTRALIA AND
INDIA AT MELBOURNE
CRICKET GROUND IN 2014.
(QUINN ROONEY-CA/CRICKET
AUSTRALIA/GETTY IMAGES)

*Possessing a fabulous sense of humour, Bill
Lawry was one of the nation's favourite
cricket commentators on Channel Nine. His
enthusiasm was infectious. In commentary
his love of Victoria and Victorian cricketers
came to the fore. He once said he would
have loved to have been a sole selector for
the Victorian State team. And, I suspect, the
same for the national side.*

*A warm, generous human being,
Bill Lawry was a great cricketer and,
I believe, he is today a national treasure
of the sporting kind.*
   — Ashley Mallett

ACKNOWLEDGEMENTS & SOURCES

The publishers would like to thank the many writers, journalists, commentators, cricketers, newspapers, online services, publishers, photographers and picture libraries who have assisted in putting this anthology together.

In particular we would like to thank Bob Bagchi, Greg Chappell, Paul Connelly, Trent Dalton, Neil Harvey, Ian Healy, Malcolm Knox, Max Kruger, Ashley Mallett, Graham McKenzie, Sidharth Monga, Barry Morrison, Roland Perry, Ken Piesse, Ian Redpath, Wayne Robinson, Tom Ryan, Anthony Sharwood, Bob Simpson, Keith Stackpole, Doug Stewart, SB Tang, and Martin Williamson.

The extracts from Wisden Cricketers' Almanack are reproduced by kind permission of John Wisden & Co Ltd.

Bob Bagchi's 'Bill Lawry – the voice of Australian summers' is reproduced with the kind permission of the *Telegraph*.

BOOKS

Benaud, Richie *My Spin on Cricket*, Hodder & Stoughton, 2005
Benaud, Richie *Willow Patterns*, Hodder & Stoughton, 1969
Greig, Joyce & Mark *Tony Greig: Love, war and cricket, a family memoir*, Pan Macmillan Australia 2013
Knox, Malcolm *The Captains: The story behind Australia's second most important job*, Hardie Grant Books, 2010
Perry, Roland *Captain Australia: A history of the celebrated captains of Australian Test cricket*, Random House, 2000
Phillipson, Neill *The Australin Cricket Hall of Fame: Great Australian cricketers past and present*, Outback Press 1979
Piesse, Ken *Dynamic Duos: Cricket's finest pairs and partnerships*, The Five Mile Press, 2012

The publishers have made all efforts to seek copyright permissions, however the publishers apologise if any copyright holder has been inadvertently overlooked or has been unable to be located.

BILL LAWRY SPEAKING AT THE MEMORIAL SERVICE FOR TONY GREIG, SYDNEY CRICKET GROUND 2013.
(BRENDON THORNE/GETTY IMAGES)